one year daily devotional for students

quiettime

the scripture cannot be broken

Quiet Time
One year daily devotional for students

Word of Life Local Church Ministries
A division of Word of Life Fellowship, Inc.
- Joe Jordan – Executive Director
- Jack Wyrtzen & Harry Bollback - Founders
- Mike Calhoun – VP of Local Church Ministries

USA
P.O. Box 600
Schroon Lake, NY 12870
talk@wol.org
1-888-932-5827

Web Address: www.wol.org

Canada
RR#8/Owen Sound
ON, Canada N4K 5W4
LCM@wol.ca
1-800-461-3503 or
(519) 376-3516

Publisher's Acknowledgements
Writers and Contributors:

Bobby Barton	1 & 2 Kings
Matt Boutilier	Hebrews
Cory Fehr	Esther, Song of Solomon, Titus, Philemon, 2 Timothy, Nahum, Malachi
Andy Grenier	Psalms, Proverbs
Paul O'Bradovic	Revelation
Joe and Gloria Phillips	John, Ephesians, Lamentations
Matt Walls	1 Corinthians

Editor: Dale Flynn
Curriculum Manager: Don Reichard
Cover and page design: Adam Rushlow

© 2007 All rights reserved. Published by Word of Life Local Church Ministries. A division of Word of Life Fellowship, Inc. The purpose of Word of Life Fellowship worldwide is the evangelization and discipleship of youth through various means consistent with the Holy Scriptures to strengthen the church of Jesus Christ. No portion of this publication may be reproduced in any form without prior written permission of the publisher.

ISBN - 978-1-931235-61-7
Printed in the United States of America

Helpful Hints For a Daily Quiet Time

The purpose of this Quiet Time is to meet the needs of spiritual growth in the life of the Christian in such a way that they learn the art of conducting their own personal investigation into the Bible. Consider the following helpful hints:

1 Give priority in choosing your quiet time. This will vary with each individual in accordance with his own circumstances. The time you choose must:
- have top priority over everything else
- be the quietest time possible.
- be a convenient time of the day or night.
- be consistently observed each day.

2 Give attention to the procedure suggested for you to follow. Include the following items.
- Read God's Word.
- Mark your Bible as you read. Here are some suggestions that might be helpful:
  a. After you read the passage put an exclamation mark next to the verses you completely understand.
  b. Put a question mark next to verses you do not understand.
  c. Put an arrow pointing upward next to encouraging verses.
  d. Put an arrow pointing downward next to verses which weigh us down in our spiritual race.
  e. Put a star next to verses containing important truths or major points.
- Meditate on what you have read (In one sentence, write the main thought). Here are some suggestions as guidelines for meditating on God's Word:

a. Look at the selected passage from God's point of view.
b. Though we encourage quiet time in the morning, some people arrange to have their quiet time at the end of their day. God emphasizes that we need to go to sleep meditating on His Word. "My soul shall be satisfied and my mouth shall praise thee with joyful lips: when I remember thee upon my bed, and meditating on thee in the night watches" (Psalm 63:5,6).
c. Deuteronomy 6:7 lists routine things you do each day during which you should concentrate on the portion of Scripture for that day:
   — when you sit in your house (meals and relaxation)
   — when you walk in the way (to and from school or work)
   — when you lie down (before going to sleep at night)
   — when you rise up (getting ready for the day)

Apply some truth to your life. (Use first person pronouns I, me, my, mine). If you have difficulty in finding an application for your life, think of yourself as a Bible SPECTator and ask yourself the following questions.

S – is there any sin for me to forsake?
P – is there any promise for me to claim?
E – is there any example for me to follow?
C – is there any command for me to obey?
T – is there anything to be thankful for today?

Pray for specific things (Use the prayer sheets found in the Personal Prayer Diary section).

3 Be sure to fill out your quiet time sheets. This will really help you remember the things the Lord brings to your mind.

4 Purpose to share with someone else each day something you gained from your quiet time. This can be a real blessing for them as well as for you.

Step by step through your Quiet Time

The Quiet Time for Students will help you have a special time each day with the Lord. The daily passages are organized so that you cover every book of the Bible in six years. All word of Life Quiet Times use the same daily passage for all ages so families, small groups, or even entire Churches can encourage each other from the Word of God.

The following examples will walk you through the steps to take to have a daily quiet time.

> First read the weekly overview to learn what the focus is for the coming week.

> Use this area to write prayer requests and reminders for the week.

> Next, listen to the Lord as you read the daily passage.

> Now share your thoughts as you answer the two questions.

qt WEEK 22

Why is it important to know what you believe and why you believe? That is a good question, and this week God is going to show why doctrine is important to our Christian life. In addition, this week Jesus deals with the question of divorce. Do you want to know where God stands on the issue? Don't miss this week!

Prayer focus for this week

Q: The Question
A: The Answer

What is the writer saying? How can I apply this to my life?

Sunday • Matthew 16:1-12

DIGGING DEEPER • There may be nothing more enjoyable to eat than freshly baked bread soaked in butter. In baking the bread, the yeast is very important. If there is too much yeast, the bread will overflow the pan and be ruined. It is not enough yeast,

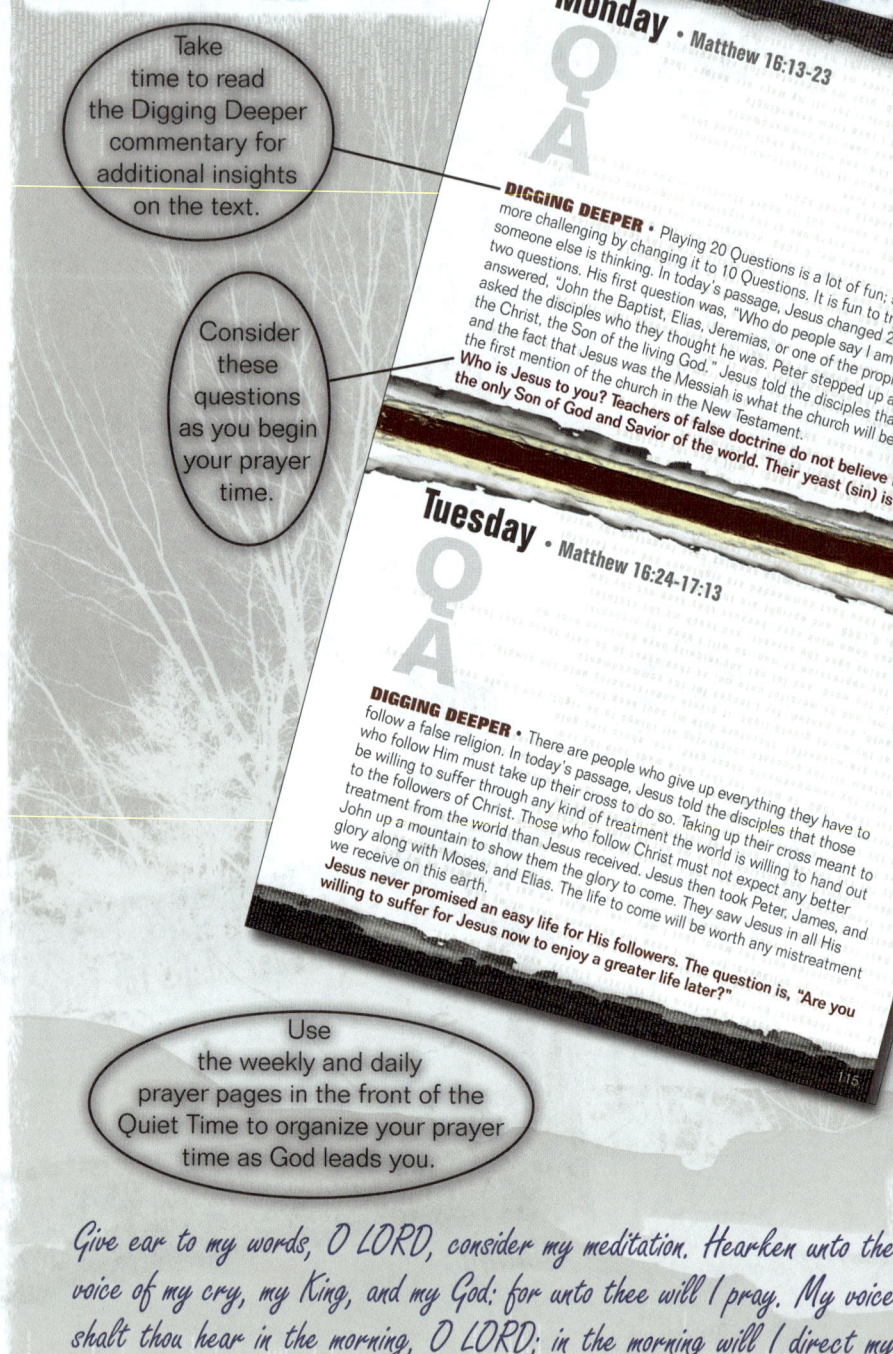

Take time to read the Digging Deeper commentary for additional insights on the text.

Consider these questions as you begin your prayer time.

Monday • Matthew 16:13-23

Q / A

DIGGING DEEPER • Playing 20 Questions is a lot of fun; so more challenging by changing it to 10 Questions. It is fun to try someone else is thinking. In today's passage, Jesus changed 20 two questions. His first question was, "Who do people say I am?" answered, "John the Baptist, Elias, Jeremias, or one of the prophe asked the disciples who they thought he was. Peter stepped up an the Christ, the Son of the living God." Jesus told the disciples that and the fact that Jesus was the Messiah is what the church will be the first mention of the church in the New Testament.

Who is Jesus to you? Teachers of false doctrine do not believe th the only Son of God and Savior of the world. Their yeast (sin) is s

Tuesday • Matthew 16:24-17:13

Q / A

DIGGING DEEPER • There are people who give up everything they have to follow a false religion. In today's passage, Jesus told the disciples that those who follow Him must take up their cross to do so. Taking up their cross meant to be willing to suffer through any kind of treatment the world is willing to hand out to the followers of Christ. Those who follow Christ must not expect any better treatment from the world than Jesus received. Jesus then took Peter, James, and John up a mountain to show them the glory to come. They saw Jesus in all His glory along with Moses, and Elias. The life to come will be worth any mistreatment we receive on this earth.

Jesus never promised an easy life for His followers. The question is, "Are you willing to suffer for Jesus now to enjoy a greater life later?"

Use the weekly and daily prayer pages in the front of the Quiet Time to organize your prayer time as God leads you.

Give ear to my words, O LORD, consider my meditation. Hearken unto the voice of my cry, my King, and my God: for unto thee will I pray. My voice shalt thou hear in the morning, O LORD; in the morning will I direct my prayer unto thee, and will look up.

Psalm 5:1-3

Sunday

Family

Christian Friends

JJ - competiveness dont let it get the best of him.

Worry - money

opening up / being able to share

Unsaved Friends

Missionaries

Monday

Family

Christian Friends

Unsaved Friends

Missionaries

Tuesday

Family

Christian Friends

Unsaved Friends

Missionaries

Wednesday

Family

Christian Friends

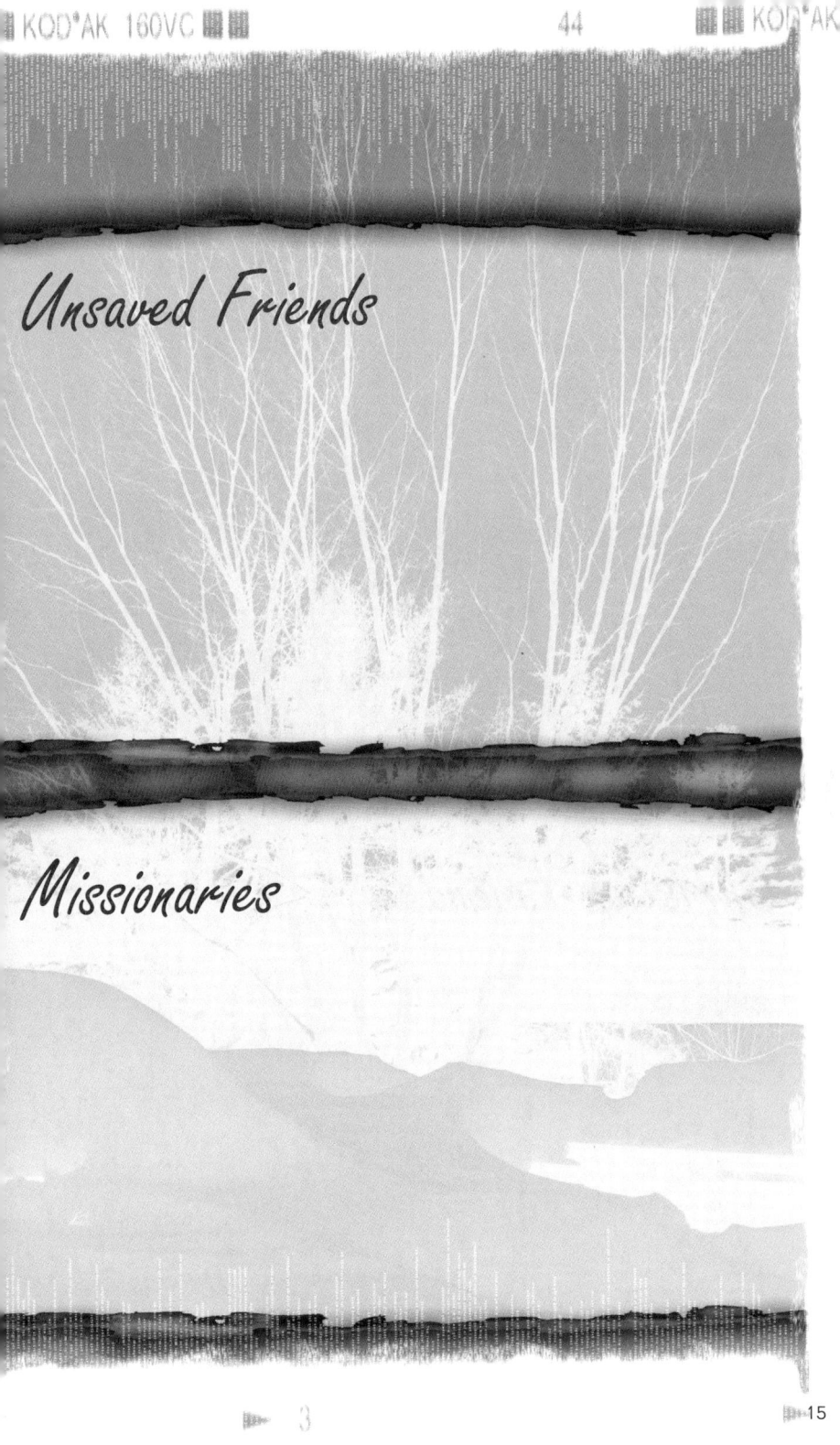

Unsaved Friends

Missionaries

Thursday

Family

Christian Friends

Unsaved Friends

Missionaries

Friday

Family

Christian Friends

Unsaved Friends

Missionaries

Saturday

Family

Christian Friends

Unsaved Friends

Missionaries

Praise List

date / answer

Praise List

date / answer

Praise List
date / answer

Praise List

date / answer

Praise List

date / answer

Something for everyone

Some people just can't get enough! That is why we have several dimensions in the Word of Life Quiet Time. Along with the daily reading, content and application questions for each day, two reading programs are given to help you understand the Bible better. Choose one or both.

Reading Through the New Testament Four Times In One Year

Turn the page and discover a schedule that takes you through the New Testament four times in one year. This is a great method to help you see the correlation of the Gospels and other New Testament books.

Reading Through the Whole Bible In One Year

Turn another page and find a program of several pages that will guide you through a chronological reading of the entire Bible. Follow this schedule and you will move from Genesis through Revelation in one year.

The Choice is Up to You

Whether you have a short quiet time, a quiet time with more scripture reading or one with a mini-Bible study each day, we trust your time with God will draw you closer to Him in every area of your life.

Read through the new testament four times in one year

Weeks 1-13

- [ ] Matthew 1-3
- [ ] Matthew 4-6
- [ ] Matthew 7-9
- [ ] Matt. 10-12
- [ ] Matt. 13-15
- [ ] Matt. 16-18
- [ ] Matt. 19-21
- [ ] Matt. 22-24
- [ ] Matt. 25-26
- [ ] Matt. 27-28
- [ ] Mark 1-3
- [ ] Mark 4-5
- [ ] Mark 6-8
- [ ] Mark 9-11
- [ ] Mark 12-14
- [ ] Mark 15-16
- [ ] Luke 1-2
- [ ] Luke 3-5
- [ ] Luke 6-7
- [ ] Luke 8-9
- [ ] Luke 10-11
- [ ] Luke 12-14
- [ ] Luke 15-17
- [ ] Luke 18-20
- [ ] Luke 21-22
- [ ] Luke 23-24
- [ ] John 1-3
- [ ] John 4-5
- [ ] John 6-7
- [ ] John 8-10
- [ ] John 11-12
- [ ] John 13-15
- [ ] John 16-18
- [ ] John 19-21
- [ ] Acts 1-3
- [ ] Acts 4-6
- [ ] Acts 7-8
- [ ] Acts 9-11
- [ ] Acts 12-15
- [ ] Acts 16-18
- [ ] Acts 19-21
- [ ] Acts 22-24
- [ ] Acts 25-26
- [ ] Acts 27-28
- [ ] Romans 1-3
- [ ] Romans 4-6
- [ ] Romans 7-9
- [ ] Romans 10-12
- [ ] Romans 13-16
- [ ] 1 Cor. 1-4
- [ ] 1 Cor. 5-9
- [ ] 1 Cor. 10-12
- [ ] 1 Cor. 13-16
- [ ] 2 Cor. 1-4
- [ ] 2 Cor. 5-8
- [ ] 2 Cor. 9-13
- [ ] Galatians 1-3
- [ ] Galatians 4-6
- [ ] Ephesians 1-3
- [ ] Ephesians 4-6
- [ ] Philippians 1-4
- [ ] Colossians 1-4
- [ ] 1 Thes. 1-3
- [ ] 1 Thes. 4-5
- [ ] 2 Thes. 1-3
- [ ] 1 Timothy 1-3
- [ ] 1 Timothy 4-6
- [ ] 2 Timothy 1-4
- [ ] Titus 1-3
- [ ] Philemon
- [ ] Hebrews 1
- [ ] Hebrews 2-4
- [ ] Hebrews 5-7
- [ ] Hebrews 8-10
- [ ] Hebrews 11-13
- [ ] James 1-3
- [ ] James 4-5
- [ ] 1 Peter 1-3
- [ ] 1 Peter 4-5
- [ ] 2 Peter 1-3
- [ ] 1 John 1-3
- [ ] 1 John 4-5
- [ ] 2 Jn, 3 Jn, Jude
- [ ] Revelation 1-3
- [ ] Revelation 4-6
- [ ] Revelation 7-9
- [ ] Rev. 10-12
- [ ] Rev. 13-15
- [ ] Rev. 16-18
- [ ] Rev. 19-22

Weeks 14-26

- [ ] Matthew 1-3
- [ ] Matthew 4-6
- [ ] Matthew 7-9
- [ ] Matt. 10-12
- [ ] Matt. 13-15
- [ ] Matt. 16-18
- [ ] Matt. 19-21
- [ ] Matt. 22-24
- [ ] Matt. 25-26
- [ ] Matt. 27-28
- [ ] Mark 1-3
- [ ] Mark 4-5
- [ ] Mark 6-8
- [ ] Mark 9-11
- [ ] Mark 12-14
- [ ] Mark 15-16
- [ ] Luke 1-2
- [ ] Luke 3-5
- [ ] Luke 6-7
- [ ] Luke 8-9
- [ ] Luke 10-11
- [ ] Luke 12-14
- [ ] Luke 15-17
- [ ] Luke 18-20
- [ ] Luke 21-22
- [ ] Luke 23-24
- [ ] John 1-3
- [ ] John 4-5
- [ ] John 6-7
- [ ] John 8-10
- [ ] John 11-12
- [ ] John 13-15
- [ ] John 16-18
- [ ] John 19-21
- [ ] Acts 1-3
- [ ] Acts 4-6
- [ ] Acts 7-8
- [ ] Acts 9-11
- [ ] Acts 12-15
- [ ] Acts 16-18
- [ ] Acts 19-21
- [ ] Acts 22-24
- [ ] Acts 25-26
- [ ] Acts 27-28
- [ ] Romans 1-3
- [ ] Romans 4-6
- [ ] Romans 7-9
- [ ] Romans 10-12
- [ ] Romans 13-16
- [ ] 1 Cor. 1-4
- [ ] 1 Cor. 5-9
- [ ] 1 Cor. 10-12
- [ ] 1 Cor. 13-16
- [ ] 2 Cor. 1-4
- [ ] 2 Cor. 5-8
- [ ] 2 Cor. 9-13
- [ ] Galatians 1-3
- [ ] Galatians 4-6
- [ ] Ephesians 1-3
- [ ] Ephesians 4-6
- [ ] Philippians 1-4
- [ ] Colossians 1-4
- [ ] 1 Thes. 1-3
- [ ] 1 Thes. 4-5
- [ ] 2 Thes. 1-3
- [ ] 1 Timothy 1-3
- [ ] 1 Timothy 4-6
- [ ] 2 Timothy 1-4
- [ ] Titus 1-3
- [ ] Philemon
- [ ] Hebrews 1
- [ ] Hebrews 2-4
- [ ] Hebrews 5-7
- [ ] Hebrews 8-10
- [ ] Hebrews 11-13
- [ ] James 1-3
- [ ] James 4-5
- [ ] 1 Peter 1-3
- [ ] 1 Peter 4-5
- [ ] 2 Peter 1-3
- [ ] 1 John 1-3
- [ ] 1 John 4-5
- [ ] 2 Jn, 3 Jn, Jude
- [ ] Revelation 1-3
- [ ] Revelation 4-6
- [ ] Revelation 7-9
- [ ] Rev. 10-12
- [ ] Rev. 13-15
- [ ] Rev. 16-18
- [ ] Rev. 19-22

Read through the new testament four times in one year

Weeks 27-39

- [ ] Matthew 1-3
- [ ] Matthew 4-6
- [ ] Matthew 7-9
- [ ] Matt. 10-12
- [ ] Matt. 13-15
- [ ] Matt. 16-18
- [ ] Matt. 19-21
- [ ] Matt. 22-24
- [ ] Matt. 25-26
- [ ] Matt. 27-28
- [ ] Mark 1-3
- [ ] Mark 4-5
- [ ] Mark 6-8
- [ ] Mark 9-11
- [ ] Mark 12-14
- [ ] Mark 15-16
- [ ] Luke 1-2
- [ ] Luke 3-5
- [ ] Luke 6-7
- [ ] Luke 8-9
- [ ] Luke 10-11
- [ ] Luke 12-14
- [ ] Luke 15-17
- [ ] Luke 18-20
- [ ] Luke 21-22
- [ ] Luke 23-24
- [ ] John 1-3
- [ ] John 4-5
- [ ] John 6-7
- [ ] John 8-10
- [ ] John 11-12
- [ ] John 13-15
- [ ] John 16-18
- [ ] John 19-21
- [ ] Acts 1-3
- [ ] Acts 4-6
- [ ] Acts 7-8
- [ ] Acts 9-11
- [ ] Acts 12-15
- [ ] Acts 16-18
- [ ] Acts 19-21
- [ ] Acts 22-24
- [ ] Acts 25-26
- [ ] Acts 27-28
- [ ] Romans 1-3
- [ ] Romans 4-6
- [ ] Romans 7-9
- [ ] Romans 10-12
- [ ] Romans 13-16
- [ ] 1 Cor. 1-4
- [ ] 1 Cor. 5-9
- [ ] 1 Cor. 10-12
- [ ] 1 Cor. 13-16
- [ ] 2 Cor. 1-4
- [ ] 2 Cor. 5-8
- [ ] 2 Cor. 9-13
- [ ] Galatians 1-3
- [ ] Galatians 4-6
- [ ] Ephesians 1-3
- [ ] Ephesians 4-6
- [ ] Phil. 1-4
- [ ] Colossians 1-4
- [ ] 1 Thes. 1-3
- [ ] 1 Thes. 4-5
- [ ] 2 Thes. 1-3
- [ ] 1 Timothy 1-3
- [ ] 1 Timothy 4-6
- [ ] 2 Timothy 1-4
- [ ] Titus 1-3
- [ ] Philemon
- [ ] Hebrews 1
- [ ] Hebrews 2-4
- [ ] Hebrews 5-7
- [ ] Hebrews 8-10
- [ ] Hebrews 11-13
- [ ] James 1-3
- [ ] James 4-5
- [ ] 1 Peter 1-3
- [ ] 1 Peter 4-5
- [ ] 2 Peter 1-3
- [ ] 1 John 1-3
- [ ] 1 John 4-5
- [ ] 2 Jn, 3 Jn, Jude
- [ ] Revelation 1-3
- [ ] Revelation 4-6
- [ ] Revelation 7-9
- [ ] Rev. 10-12
- [ ] Rev. 13-15
- [ ] Rev. 16-18
- [ ] Rev. 19-22

Weeks 40-52

- [ ] Matthew 1-3
- [ ] Matthew 4-6
- [ ] Matthew 7-9
- [ ] Matt. 10-12
- [ ] Matt. 13-15
- [ ] Matt. 16-18
- [ ] Matt. 19-21
- [ ] Matt. 22-24
- [ ] Matt. 25-26
- [ ] Matt. 27-28
- [ ] Mark 1-3
- [ ] Mark 4-5
- [ ] Mark 6-8
- [ ] Mark 9-11
- [ ] Mark 12-14
- [ ] Mark 15-16
- [ ] Luke 1-2
- [ ] Luke 3-5
- [ ] Luke 6-7
- [ ] Luke 8-9
- [ ] Luke 10-11
- [ ] Luke 12-14
- [ ] Luke 15-17
- [ ] Luke 18-20
- [ ] Luke 21-22
- [ ] Luke 23-24
- [ ] John 1-3
- [ ] John 4-5
- [ ] John 6-7
- [ ] John 8-10
- [ ] John 11-12
- [ ] John 13-15
- [ ] John 16-18
- [ ] John 19-21
- [ ] Acts 1-3
- [ ] Acts 4-6
- [ ] Acts 7-8
- [ ] Acts 9-11
- [ ] Acts 12-15
- [ ] Acts 16-18
- [ ] Acts 19-21
- [ ] Acts 22-24
- [ ] Acts 25-26
- [ ] Acts 27-28
- [ ] Romans 1-3
- [ ] Romans 4-6
- [ ] Romans 7-9
- [ ] Romans 10-12
- [ ] Romans 13-16
- [ ] 1 Cor. 1-4
- [ ] 1 Cor. 5-9
- [ ] 1 Cor. 10-12
- [ ] 1 Cor. 13-16
- [ ] 2 Cor. 1-4
- [ ] 2 Cor. 5-8
- [ ] 2 Cor. 9-13
- [ ] Galatians 1-3
- [ ] Galatians 4-6
- [ ] Ephesians 1-3
- [ ] Ephesians 4-6
- [ ] Phil. 1-4
- [ ] Colossians 1-4
- [ ] 1 Thes. 1-3
- [ ] 1 Thes. 4-5
- [ ] 2 Thes. 1-3
- [ ] 1 Timothy 1-3
- [ ] 1 Timothy 4-6
- [ ] 2 Timothy 1-4
- [ ] Titus 1-3
- [ ] Philemon
- [ ] Hebrews 1
- [ ] Hebrews 2-4
- [ ] Hebrews 5-7
- [ ] Hebrews 8-10
- [ ] Hebrews 11-13
- [ ] James 1-3
- [ ] James 4-5
- [ ] 1 Peter 1-3
- [ ] 1 Peter 4-5
- [ ] 2 Peter 1-3
- [ ] 1 John 1-3
- [ ] 1 John 4-5
- [ ] 2 Jn, 3 Jn, Jude
- [ ] Revelation 1-3
- [ ] Revelation 4-6
- [ ] Revelation 7-9
- [ ] Rev. 10-12
- [ ] Rev. 13-15
- [ ] Rev. 16-18
- [ ] Rev. 19-22

Bible reading schedule

Read through the Bible in one year! As you complete each daily reading, simply place a check in the appropriate box.

- [ ] 1 Genesis 1-3
- [ ] 2 Genesis 4:1-6:8
- [ ] 3 Genesis 6:9-9:29
- [ ] 4 Genesis 10-11
- [ ] 5 Genesis 12-14
- [ ] 6 Genesis 15-17
- [ ] 7 Genesis 18-19
- [ ] 8 Genesis 20-22
- [ ] 9 Genesis 23-24
- [ ] 10 Genesis 25-26
- [ ] 11 Genesis 27-28
- [ ] 12 Genesis 29-30
- [ ] 13 Genesis 31-32
- [ ] 14 Genesis 33-35
- [ ] 15 Genesis 36-37
- [ ] 16 Genesis 38-40
- [ ] 17 Genesis 41-42
- [ ] 18 Genesis 43-45
- [ ] 19 Genesis 46-47
- [ ] 20 Genesis 48-50
- [ ] 21 Job 1-3
- [ ] 22 Job 4-7
- [ ] 23 Job 8-11
- [ ] 24 Job 12-15
- [ ] 25 Job 16-19
- [ ] 26 Job 20-22
- [ ] 27 Job 23-28
- [ ] 28 Job 29-31
- [ ] 29 Job 32-34
- [ ] 30 Job 35-37
- [ ] 31 Job 38-42
- [ ] 32 Exodus 1-4
- [ ] 33 Exodus 5-8
- [ ] 34 Exodus 9-11
- [ ] 35 Exodus 12-13
- [ ] 36 Exodus 14-15
- [ ] 37 Exodus 16-18
- [ ] 38 Exodus 19-21
- [ ] 39 Exodus 22-24
- [ ] 40 Exodus 25-27
- [ ] 41 Exodus 28-29
- [ ] 42 Exodus 30-31
- [ ] 43 Exodus 32-34
- [ ] 44 Exodus 35-36
- [ ] 45 Exodus 37-38
- [ ] 46 Exodus 39-40
- [ ] 47 Leviticus 1:1-5:13
- [ ] 48 Leviticus 5:14-7:38
- [ ] 49 Leviticus 8-10
- [ ] 50 Leviticus 11-12
- [ ] 51 Leviticus 13-14
- [ ] 52 Leviticus 15-17
- [ ] 53 Leviticus 18-20
- [ ] 54 Leviticus 21-23
- [ ] 55 Leviticus 24-25
- [ ] 56 Leviticus 26-27
- [ ] 57 Numbers 1-2
- [ ] 58 Numbers 3-4
- [ ] 59 Numbers 5-6
- [ ] 60 Numbers 7
- [ ] 61 Numbers 8-10
- [ ] 62 Numbers 11-13
- [ ] 63 Numbers 14-15
- [ ] 64 Numbers 16-18
- [ ] 65 Numbers 19-21
- [ ] 66 Numbers 22-24
- [ ] 67 Numbers 25-26
- [ ] 68 Numbers 27-29
- [ ] 69 Numbers 30-31
- [ ] 70 Numbers 32-33
- [ ] 71 Numbers 34-36
- [ ] 72 Deuteronomy 1-2
- [ ] 73 Deuteronomy 3-4
- [ ] 74 Deuteronomy 5-7
- [ ] 75 Deuteronomy 8-10
- [ ] 76 Deuteronomy 11-13
- [ ] 77 Deuteronomy 14-17
- [ ] 78 Deuteronomy 18-21
- [ ] 79 Deuteronomy 22-25
- [ ] 80 Deuteronomy 26-28
- [ ] 81 Deuteronomy 29:1-31:29
- [ ] 82 Deuteronomy 31:30-34:12
- [ ] 83 Joshua 1-4
- [ ] 84 Joshua 5-8
- [ ] 85 Joshua 9-11
- [ ] 86 Joshua 12-14
- [ ] 87 Joshua 15-17
- [ ] 88 Joshua 18-19
- [ ] 89 Joshua 20-22
- [ ] 90 Joshua 23 - Judges 1
- [ ] 91 Judges 2-5
- [ ] 92 Judges 6-8
- [ ] 93 Judges 9
- [ ] 94 Judges 10-12
- [ ] 95 Judges 13-16
- [ ] 96 Judges 17-19
- [ ] 97 Judges 20-21
- [ ] 98 Ruth
- [ ] 99 1 Samuel 1-3
- [ ] 100 1 Samuel 4-7
- [ ] 101 1 Samuel 8-10
- [ ] 102 1 Samuel 11-13
- [ ] 103 1 Samuel 14-15
- [ ] 104 1 Samuel 16-17

Bible reading schedule
Day 105 - 199

- [ ] 105 1 Samuel 18-19; Psalm 59
- [ ] 106 1 Samuel 20-21; Psalm 56; 34
- [ ] 107 1 Samuel 22-23; 1 Chronicles 12:8-18; Psalm 52; 54; 63; 142
- [ ] 108 1 Samuel 24; Psalm 57; 1 Samuel 25
- [ ] 109 1 Samuel 26-29; 1 Chronicles 12:1-7, 19-22
- [ ] 110 1 Samuel 30-31; 1 Chronicles 10; 2 Samuel 1
- [ ] 111 2 Samuel 2-4
- [ ] 112 2 Samuel 5:1-6:11; 1 Chronicles 11:1-9; 2:23-40; 13:1-14:17
- [ ] 113 2 Samuel 22; Psalm 18
- [ ] 114 1 Chronicles 15-16; 2 Samuel 6:12-23; Psalm 96
- [ ] 115 Psalm 105; 2 Samuel 7; 1 Chronicles 17
- [ ] 116 2 Samuel 8-10; 1 Chronicles 18-19; Psalm 60
- [ ] 117 2 Samuel 11-12; 1 Chronicles 20:1-3; Psalm 51
- [ ] 118 2 Samuel 13-14
- [ ] 119 2 Samuel 15-17
- [ ] 120 Psalm 3; 2 Samuel 18-19
- [ ] 121 2 Samuel 20-21; 23:8-23; 1 Chronicles 20:4-8; 11:10-25
- [ ] 122 2 Samuel 23:24-24:25;
- [ ] 123 1 Chronicles 11:26-47; 21:1-30, 1 Chronicles 22-24
- [ ] 124 Psalm 30; 1 Chronicles 25-26
- [ ] 125 1 Chronicles 27-29
- [ ] 126 Psalms 5-7; 10; 11; 13; 17
- [ ] 127 Psalms 23; 26; 28; 31; 35
- [ ] 128 Psalms 41; 43; 46; 55; 61; 62; 64
- [ ] 129 Psalms 69-71; 77
- [ ] 130 Psalms 83; 86; 88; 91; 95
- [ ] 131 Psalms 108-9; 120-21; 140; 143-44
- [ ] 132 Psalms 1; 14-15; 36-37; 39
- [ ] 133 Psalms 40; 49-50; 73
- [ ] 134 Psalms 76; 82; 84; 90; 92; 112; 115
- [ ] 135 Psalms 8-9; 16; 19; 21; 24; 29
- [ ] 136 Psalms 33; 65-68
- [ ] 137 Psalms 75; 93-94; 97-100
- [ ] 138 Psalms 103-4; 113-14; 117
- [ ] 139 Psalm 119:1-88
- [ ] 140 Psalm 119:89-176
- [ ] 141 Psalms 122; 124; 133-36
- [ ] 142 Psalms 138-39; 145; 148; 150
- [ ] 143 Psalms 4; 12; 20; 25; 32; 38
- [ ] 144 Psalms 42; 53; 58; 81; 101; 111; 130-31; 141; 146
- [ ] 145 Psalms 2; 22; 27
- [ ] 146 Psalms 45; 47-48; 87; 110
- [ ] 147 1 Kings 1:1-2:12; 2 Samuel 23:1-7
- [ ] 148 1 Kings 2:13-3:28; 2 Chronicles 1:1-13
- [ ] 149 1 Kings 5-6; 2 Chronicles 2-3
- [ ] 150 1 Kings 7; 2 Chronicles 4
- [ ] 151 1 Kings 8; 2 Chronicles 5:1-7:10
- [ ] 152 1 Kings 9:1-10:13; 2 Chronicles 7:11-9:12
- [ ] 153 1 Kings 4; 10:14-29; 2 Chronicles 1:14-17; 9:13-28; Psalm 72
- [ ] 154 Proverbs 1-3
- [ ] 155 Proverbs 4-6
- [ ] 156 Proverbs 7-9
- [ ] 157 Proverbs 10-12
- [ ] 158 Proverbs 13-15
- [ ] 159 Proverbs 16-18
- [ ] 160 Proverbs 19-21
- [ ] 161 Proverbs 22-24
- [ ] 162 Proverbs 25-27
- [ ] 163 Proverbs 28-29
- [ ] 164 Proverbs 30-31; Psalm 127
- [ ] 165 Song of Solomon
- [ ] 166 1 Kings 11:1-40; Ecclesiastes 1-2
- [ ] 167 Ecclesiastes 3-7
- [ ] 168 Ecclesiastes 8-12; 1 Kings 11:41-43; 2 Chronicles 9:29-31
- [ ] 169 1 Kings 12; 2 Chronicles 10:1-11:17
- [ ] 170 1 Kings 13-14; 2 Chronicles 11:18-12:16
- [ ] 171 1 Kings 15:1-24; 2 Chronicles 13-16
- [ ] 172 1 Kings 15:25-16:34; 2 Chronicles 17; 1 Kings 17
- [ ] 173 1 Kings 18-19
- [ ] 174 1 Kings 20-21
- [ ] 175 1 Kings 22:1-40; 2 Chronicles 18
- [ ] 176 1 Kings 22:41-53; 2 Kings 1; 2 Chronicles 19:1-21:3
- [ ] 177 2 Kings 2-4
- [ ] 178 2 Kings 5-7
- [ ] 179 2 Kings 8-9; 2 Chronicles 21:4-22:9
- [ ] 180 2 Kings 10-11; 2 Chronicles 22:10-23:21
- [ ] 181 Joel
- [ ] 182 2 Kings 12-13; 2 Chronicles 24
- [ ] 183 2 Kings 14; 2 Chronicles 25; Jonah
- [ ] 184 Hosea 1-7
- [ ] 185 Hosea 8-14
- [ ] 186 2 Kings 15:1-7; 2 Chronicles 26; Amos 1-4
- [ ] 187 Amos 5-9; 2 Kings 15:8-18
- [ ] 188 Isaiah 1-4
- [ ] 189 2 Kings 15:19-38; 2 Chronicles 27; Isaiah 5-6
- [ ] 190 Micah
- [ ] 191 2 Kings 16; 2 Chronicles 28; Isaiah 7-8
- [ ] 192 Isaiah 9-12
- [ ] 193 Isaiah 13-16
- [ ] 194 Isaiah 17-22
- [ ] 195 Isaiah 23-27
- [ ] 196 Isaiah 28-30
- [ ] 197 Isaiah 31-35
- [ ] 198 2 Kings 18:1-8; 2 Chronicles 29-31
- [ ] 199 2 Kings 17; 18:9-37; 2 Chronicles 32:1-19; Isaiah 36

Bible reading schedule
Day 200 - 288

- [ ] 200 2 Kings 19; 2 Chronicles 32:20-23; Isaiah 37
- [ ] 201 2 Kings 20; 2 Chronicles 32:24-33; Isaiah 38-39
- [ ] 202 2 Kings 21:1-18; 2 Chronicles 33:1-20; Isaiah 40
- [ ] 203 Isaiah 41-43
- [ ] 204 Isaiah 44-47
- [ ] 205 Isaiah 48-51
- [ ] 206 Isaiah 52-57
- [ ] 207 Isaiah 58-62
- [ ] 208 Isaiah 63-66
- [ ] 209 2 Kings 21:19-26; 2 Chronicles 33:21-34:7; Zephaniah
- [ ] 210 Jeremiah 1-3
- [ ] 211 Jeremiah 4-6
- [ ] 212 Jeremiah 7-9
- [ ] 213 Jeremiah 10-13
- [ ] 214 Jeremiah 14-16
- [ ] 215 Jeremiah 17-20
- [ ] 216 2 Kings 22:1-23:28; 2 Chronicles 34:8-35:19
- [ ] 217 Nahum; 2 Kings 23:29-37; 2 Chronicles 35:20-36:5; Jeremiah 22:10-17
- [ ] 218 Jeremiah 26; Habakkuk
- [ ] 219 Jeremiah 46-47; 2 Kings 24:1-4, 7; 2 Chronicles 36:6-7; Jeremiah 25, 35
- [ ] 220 Jeremiah 36, 45, 48
- [ ] 221 Jeremiah 49:1-33; Daniel 1-2
- [ ] 222 Jeremiah 22:18-30; 2 Kings 24:5-20; 2 Chronicles 36:8-12; Jeremiah 37:1-2; 52:1-3; 24; 29
- [ ] 223 Jeremiah 27-28, 23
- [ ] 224 Jeremiah 50-51
- [ ] 225 Jeremiah 49:34-39; 34:1-22; Ezekiel 1-3
- [ ] 226 Ezekiel 4-7
- [ ] 227 Ezekiel 8-11
- [ ] 228 Ezekiel 12-14
- [ ] 229 Ezekiel 15-17
- [ ] 230 Ezekiel 18-20
- [ ] 231 Ezekiel 21-23
- [ ] 232 2 Kings 25:1; 2 Chronicles 36:13-16; Jeremiah 39:1; 52:4; Ezekiel 24; Jeremiah 21:1-22:9; 32:1-44
- [ ] 233 Jeremiah 30-31, 33
- [ ] 234 Ezekiel 25; 29:1-16; 30; 31
- [ ] 235 Ezekiel 26-28
- [ ] 236 Jeremiah 37:3-39:10; 52:5-30; 2 Kings 25:2-21; 2 Chronicles 36:17-21
- [ ] 237 2 Kings 25:22; Jeremiah 39:11-40:6; Lamentations 1-3
- [ ] 238 Lamentations 4-5; Obadiah
- [ ] 239 Jeremiah 40:7-44:30; 2 Kings 25:23-26
- [ ] 240 Ezekiel 33:21-36:38
- [ ] 241 Ezekiel 37-39
- [ ] 242 Ezekiel 32:1-33:20; Daniel 3
- [ ] 243 Ezekiel 40-42
- [ ] 244 Ezekiel 43-45
- [ ] 245 Ezekiel 46-48
- [ ] 246 Ezekiel 29:17-21; Daniel 4; Jeremiah 52:31-34; 2 Kings 25:27-30; Psalm 44
- [ ] 247 Psalms 74; 79-80; 89
- [ ] 248 Psalms 85; 102; 106; 123; 137
- [ ] 249 Daniel 7-8; 5
- [ ] 250 Daniel 9; 6
- [ ] 251 2 Chronicles 36:22-23; Ezra 1:1-4:5
- [ ] 252 Daniel 10-12
- [ ] 253 Ezra 4:6-6:13; Haggai
- [ ] 254 Zechariah 1-6
- [ ] 255 Zechariah 7-8; Ezra 6:14-22; Psalm 78
- [ ] 256 Psalms 107; 116; 118
- [ ] 257 Psalms 125-26; 128-29; 132; 147; 149
- [ ] 258 Zechariah 9-14
- [ ] 259 Esther 1-4
- [ ] 260 Esther 5-10
- [ ] 261 Ezra 7-8
- [ ] 262 Ezra 9-10
- [ ] 263 Nehemiah 1-5
- [ ] 264 Nehemiah 6-7
- [ ] 265 Nehemiah 8-10
- [ ] 266 Nehemiah 11-13
- [ ] 267 Malachi
- [ ] 268 1 Chronicles 1-2
- [ ] 269 1 Chronicles 3-5
- [ ] 270 1 Chronicles 6
- [ ] 271 1 Chronicles 7:1-8:27
- [ ] 272 1 Chronicles 8:28-9:44
- [ ] 273 John 1:1-18; Mark 1:1; Luke 1:1-4; 3:23-38; Matthew 1:1-17
- [ ] 274 Luke 1:5-80
- [ ] 275 Matthew 1:18-2:23; Luke 2
- [ ] 276 Matthew 3:1-4:11; Mark 1:2-13; Luke 3:1-23; 4:1-13; John 1:19-34
- [ ] 277 John 1:35-3:36
- [ ] 278 John 4; Matthew 4:12-17; Mark 1:14-15; Luke 4:14-30
- [ ] 279 Mark 1:16-45; Matthew 4:18-25; 8:2-4, 14-17; Luke 4:31-5:16
- [ ] 280 Matthew 9:1-17; Mark 2:1-22; Luke 5:17-39
- [ ] 281 John 5; Matthew 12:1-21; Mark 2:23-3:12; Luke 6:1-11
- [ ] 282 Matthew 5; Mark 3:13-19; Luke 6:12-36
- [ ] 283 Matthew 6-7; Luke 6:37-49
- [ ] 284 Luke 7; Matthew 8:1, 5-13; 11:2-30
- [ ] 285 Matthew 12:22-50; Mark 3:20-35; Luke 8:1-21
- [ ] 286 Mark 4:1-34; Matthew 13:1-53
- [ ] 287 Mark 4:35-5:43; Matthew 8:18, 23-34; 9:18-34; Luke 8:22-56
- [ ] 288 Mark 6:1-30; Matthew 13:54-58; 9:35-11:1; 14:1-12; Luke 9:1-10

Bible reading schedule
Day 289 - 365

- [ ] 289 Matthew 14:13-36; Mark 6:31-56; Luke 9:11-17; John 6:1-21
- [ ] 290 John 6:22-7:1; Matthew 15:1-20; Mark 7:1-23
- [ ] 291 Matthew 15:21-16:20; Mark 7:24-8:30; Luke 9:18-21
- [ ] 292 Matthew 16:21-17:27; Mark 8:31-9:32; Luke 9:22-45
- [ ] 293 Matthew 18; 8:19-22; Mark 9:33-50; Luke 9:46-62; John 7:2-10
- [ ] 294 John 7:11-8:59
- [ ] 295 Luke 10:1-11:36
- [ ] 296 Luke 11:37-13:21
- [ ] 297 John 9-10
- [ ] 298 Luke 13:22-15:32
- [ ] 299 Luke 16:1-17:10; John 11:1-54
- [ ] 300 Luke 17:11-18:17; Matthew 19:1-15; Mark 10:1-16
- [ ] 301 Matthew 19:16-20:28; Mark 10:17-45; Luke 18:18-34
- [ ] 302 Matthew 20:29-34; 26:6-13; Mark 10:46-52; 14:3-9; Luke 18:35-19:28; John 11:55-12:11
- [ ] 303 Matthew 21:1-22; Mark 11:1-26; Luke 19:29-48; John 12:12-50
- [ ] 304 Matthew 21:23-22:14; Mark 11:27-12:12; Luke 20:1-19
- [ ] 305 Matthew 22:15-46; Mark 12:13-37; Luke 20:20-44
- [ ] 306 Matthew 23; Mark 12:38-44; Luke 20:45-21:4
- [ ] 307 Matthew 24:1-31; Mark 13:1-27; Luke 21:5-27
- [ ] 308 Matthew 24:32-26:5, 14-16; Mark 13:28-14:2, 10-11; Luke 21:28-22:6
- [ ] 309 Matthew 26:17-29; Mark 14:12-25; Luke 22:7-38; John 13
- [ ] 310 John 14-16
- [ ] 311 John 17:1-18:1; Matthew 26:30-46; Mark 14:26-42; Luke 22:39-46
- [ ] 312 Matthew 26:47-75; Mark 14:43-72; Luke 22:47-65; John 18:2-27
- [ ] 313 Matthew 27:1-26; Mark 15:1-15; Luke 22:66-23:25; John 18:28-19:16
- [ ] 314 Matthew 27:27-56; Mark 15:16-41; Luke 23:26-49; John 19:17-30
- [ ] 315 Matthew 27:57-28:8; Mark 15:42-16:8; Luke 23:50-24:12; John 19:31-20:10
- [ ] 316 Matthew 28:9-20; Mark 16:9-20; Luke 24:13-53; John 20:11-21:25
- [ ] 317 Acts 1-2
- [ ] 318 Acts 3-5
- [ ] 319 Acts 6:1-8:1
- [ ] 320 Acts 8:2-9:43
- [ ] 321 Acts 10-11
- [ ] 322 Acts 12-13
- [ ] 323 Acts 14-15
- [ ] 324 Galatians 1-3
- [ ] 325 Galatians 4-6
- [ ] 326 James
- [ ] 327 Acts 16:1-18:11
- [ ] 328 1 Thessalonians
- [ ] 329 2 Thessalonians; Acts 18:12-19:22
- [ ] 330 1 Corinthians 1-4
- [ ] 331 1 Corinthians 5-8
- [ ] 332 1 Corinthians 9-11
- [ ] 333 1 Corinthians 12-14
- [ ] 334 1 Corinthians 15-16
- [ ] 335 Acts 19:23-20:1; 2 Corinthians 1-4
- [ ] 336 2 Corinthians 5-9
- [ ] 337 2 Corinthians 10-13
- [ ] 338 Romans 1-3
- [ ] 339 Romans 4-6
- [ ] 340 Romans 7-8
- [ ] 341 Romans 9-11
- [ ] 342 Romans 12-15
- [ ] 343 Romans 16; Acts 20:2-21:16
- [ ] 344 Acts 21:17-23:35
- [ ] 345 Acts 24-26
- [ ] 346 Acts 27-28
- [ ] 347 Ephesians 1-3
- [ ] 348 Ephesians 4-6
- [ ] 349 Colossians
- [ ] 350 Philippians
- [ ] 351 Philemon; 1 Timothy 1-3
- [ ] 352 1 Timothy 4-6; Titus
- [ ] 353 2 Timothy
- [ ] 354 1 Peter
- [ ] 355 Jude; 2 Peter
- [ ] 356 Hebrews 1:1-5:10
- [ ] 357 Hebrews 5:11-9:28
- [ ] 358 Hebrews 10-11
- [ ] 359 Hebrews 12-13; 2 John; 3 John
- [ ] 360 1 John
- [ ] 361 Revelation 1-3
- [ ] 362 Revelation 4-9
- [ ] 363 Revelation 10-14
- [ ] 364 Revelation 15-18
- [ ] 365 Revelation 19-22

From the Liberty Bible, King James Version. Copyright ©1975, Thomas Nelson, Inc. Publishers. Used by permission.

qt WEEK 1

It is common for us to take for granted the faithfulness of God and His care for us. David worked through this very attitude and concluded in Psalm 27:13, "I had fainted, unless I had believed to see the goodness of the LORD in the land of the living." We should be able to agree with David by the end of this week.

Prayer focus for this week

Not having any stress, so I will be able to be happy and focus on God instead of my worries. Have God examine us so we can be forgiving.

Q: The Question — What is the writer saying?
A: The Answer — How Can I apply this to my life?

Sunday • Psalm 26:1-12

- Starting this Devotion
- Giving him my stress and worries
- Pray for the wisdom i need to do what God wants me to do, and not what I want to do.

DIGGING DEEPER • Every time a car drives over a bridge, it is a test of the integrity and strength of the structure. In verse 2, David asked God to test his heart and mind to see that he was a man of integrity and that he still walked in God's Truth. David continued his request and pointed out that he didn't keep company with idolaters, hypocrites, or the wicked. David was not ashamed of God, but publicly thanked Him and told others about His wonderful works. David committed himself to spending time with those who loved and honored the Lord, and sought to avoid violent people. David intended to live a life of integrity, and he asked God to redeem him and show him mercy, that he might be successful.
List two things God has used in your life to test your faithfulness to Him and His Word. What will you do differently the next time you are tested?

Monday • Psalm 27:1-14

DIGGING DEEPER • Every day the news tells of people around the world who fear some enemy who might destroy all that they have, kill their families, or even kill them. People beg for help and look for someone who will protect and rescue them from their enemies. David is asking just that of the Lord in today's Psalm. David expresses his trust in God from the very first verse and proclaims that he will not fear even though enemies rise up against him. David knows that God will hide him or make him feel secure in a private place of God's own choosing. David declares his hope in God and states that he would have lost heart unless he believed that he would see God's goodness.
List a time when you overcame your fear through believing in God's goodness and strength. Endeavor to tell someone else about it today.

Tuesday • Psalm 28:1-9

DIGGING DEEPER • Most of us have been falsely accused by friends, family, or someone who doesn't like us. Some of us have even experienced life-threatening actions from those who would seek to hurt or discredit us. When King David wrote this Psalm, he was in danger from his own son who was trying to take his throne. David was accused of being wicked (2 Samuel 16:8), which was the reason his enemies thought God was taking the kingdom from him. David cried out to God, asking that the people would not believe these false allegations. He also asked God to give them what they deserved as deceptive liars. David sets an example for us as he praises God. Praise is an uplifting experience that will strengthen us.
Read verses 6-9 again and list three specific times when God has given you strength to trust Him as your stronghold and refuge.

Wednesday • Psalm 29:1-11

Gives us hope
Blesses us when we don't expect it.

DIGGING DEEPER • Each of us understands the joy of hearing the voices of those we love. When our cell phone rings, we look forward to hearing their voices. When they call out our name, or announce that they are home, that sound is an instant encouragement to us. David recognizes that the voice of the LORD is such a sound. It is evidence of His majesty and power, and by His word He rules the earth. How comforting to know that our God has that kind of power and that He wants to develop a relationship with us! Verse 10 says, "The LORD sitteth King for ever." Our response to the Lord is to give Him all the glory that is due Him and to worship Him in holiness.
From this passage, list three ways the Lord strengthens and blesses us. Find someone today with whom to share a blessing God has given you.

Thursday • Psalm 30:1-12

Worked out problems w/ girlfriend
No more stress over playing volleyball
Financially good

DIGGING DEEPER • We remember the times when, as children, we needed a reminder from our parents to say "thank you" for something that was given to us or done for us. The same is true when it comes to the blessings from the Lord. David sets the example listing several reasons to extol or praise God. To start with, the Lord lifted David up (v. 1). The Lord healed him (v. 2). He delivered him from spiritual death (v. 3). He delivered him from physical death (v. 3). He established David's kingdom (v. 7). He turned his mourning into dancing, and He replaced his sorrow with gladness (v. 11). When we forget our many blessings, Satan uses that to cause us to feel sorry for ourselves and to blame God for our circumstances.
List four blessings from God you've had recently, take some time in prayer to thank Him and then tell someone else what God has done for you.

Friday • Psalm 31:1-13

DIGGING DEEPER • Even though many of us have never experienced what David did as he ran for his life from his son Absalom, the strength and character of God are always available to us. David trusted God as his rock and fortress, his strength, the One who held his time in His hand, and the One who preserves the faithful. Because of David's trust in his LORD he could say in verse 5, "Into thine hand I commit my spirit." These are nearly the same words Christ used on the cross as He died (Luke 23:46). Job also kept his eyes on the Lord during his time of trial when he said of God, "Though he slay me, yet will I trust in him" (Job 13:15). The words of Job, David, and Jesus should be proof enough that God can be trusted. **When do you find it the hardest to trust God? Why is it so hard? Pray the prayer of David and Christ, who committed themselves to God's care.**

Saturday • Psalm 31:14-24

Probaly patientce, waiting for God's timing. Wanting to do things my way instead of God's.
- *wanting answers right away*
- *not listening*

DIGGING DEEPER • The word perspective means "the capacity to view things in their true relations or relative importance" From a child's perspective, it seems that his father can do anything. To the child, the simplicity of every day life appears to be well within Dad's ability to fix whatever needs fixing. That perspective changes with age. David does not forget who God is, and he starts this section with the same evaluation of life we all should have: "My times are in thy hand." David understands his situation in the first half of this Psalm; but, more importantly, he knows where he stands with God. Our hope is in God because we are in His hand and He preserves the faithful.
In what area of your life are you most impatient? List what keeps you from trusting God in this area. Choose today to believe that God is in control.

qt WEEK 2

Whether we admit it or not, we all need God. We need His forgiveness and we need Him to be near when we are brokenhearted. We rejoice greatly that God is our Lord and our friend even when it seems that no one else is. This is a week of perspective about who our God is and the advantage that gives us.

Prayer focus for this week

For more patience in all areas of my Life. Also thanking God for everything I have. Being thankfull. Giving praise to Jesus.

Q: The Question — *What is the writer saying?*
A: The Answer — *How Can I apply this to my life?*

Sunday • Psalm 32:1-11

DIGGING DEEPER • David rejoices that his transgression (sin) has been forgiven by God. Psalm 32 was written after David's act of adultery with Bathsheba. His sin was revealed by Nathan, a prophet, in 2 Samuel 12. David's situation is a reminder for all of us who don't believe that the effects of sin are all that bad. David's bones ached like an old man, and his heart was in such grief that he groaned all day long. The convicting hand of God weighed heavily upon him until he confessed his sin. He was spiritually as dry as a summer drought. The stubborn and wicked will be visited by many sorrows; however, there is forgiveness, preservation, gladness, and rejoicing for those who confess their sins and are forgiven.

Make a list of any unconfessed sins you may have, then list any individual to whom you need to apologize. Confess and apologize, then shred the list.

Monday • Psalm 33:1-9

— He has so much power. We should fear God. Sometimes I don't think we do. — He does so much for us that we over look. Simple things like giving us air, food, water. Simple things but they are essential to survive.

DIGGING DEEPER • Now that you have confessed and destroyed yesterday's list of sins, it's time to move on in your spiritual quest. The act of confessing our sin is the beginning of the cleansing our heart needs, which John talks about in 1 John 1:9. We confess, but it is God who forgives and cleanses. Psalm 33 illustrates the natural next step of rejoicing in the Lord after we have been forgiven and cleansed from sin. Animals often splash around in the cold water of a pond in order to wash off the dust and keep cool. It looks like a party as they enjoy their relief. The joy we have in our Lord should be the same when we've confessed our sin. Oh, the joy of feeling cleansed from sin!
Read verse 8 and list five reasons you stand in awe (wonder) of God. Now pray these back to God; you'll be amazed at the feeling it gives.

Tuesday • Psalm 33:10-22

DIGGING DEEPER • When we look at the mountains that have been here forever, or trees so huge a car can drive through them, we still don't have the full picture of God's wisdom and counsel. A mountain can be destroyed by a volcano and a tree can be blown over or burned up, but God's plan and counsel stand forever. Man cannot offer shelter when God desires to intervene and deal with a person or a nation; there is no human defense against God's judgment. Yet, for the believer, the eye of the Lord is on those who hope in His mercy, and He will deliver them from defeat and death. Our natural response is found in verse 21, where the writer says that "our heart shall rejoice in him, because we have trusted in his holy name."
Talk to your youth leader and ask him for a Christian Service you can do this week, then trust the Lord to enable you to do it.

Wednesday • Psalm 34:1-10

DIGGING DEEPER • We are all familiar with the celebration that takes place when someone has just won a sporting event, an election, or a game. Children or teenagers commonly pump their fists in the air or jump around excited over their victory. David has similar emotions as he declares his joy over God's glory and deliverance. The Lord has delivered David from his fears and his troubles. He has done this by putting a hedge of defense around David, because he respects and honors (fears) God. The conclusion of the matter for David is that he will boast in the Lord, and magnify Him while enjoying God's goodness. This is having the proper fear (respect and honor) for the Lord.

Talk to an elderly Christian (Mom and Dad count) and write down some of the blessings they have experienced over the years.

Thursday • Psalm 34:11-22

DIGGING DEEPER • Most of us have asked a friend what his favorite TV program is, or the best video game to buy, or about his favorite actor or athlete. We want details, because we want to know if it is something we would be interested in, too. David recommends to his readers his Lord, who is good and faithful to everyone who is righteous. The eye of the Lord is on the righteous. The Lord hears and delivers them. He is near to the brokenhearted and saves those who are sorry for their sins. The righteous have not been promised an easy life, but we have the Lord to deliver us, for He is our redeemer. This is quite a contrast from the fate of the ungodly: "The face of the LORD is against them who do evil."

Write down the name of the last person you told about Christ and when. What can you offer from today's lesson that would be an encouragement?

Friday • Psalm 35:1-14

DIGGING DEEPER • There are many times when we are disappointed and frustrated with people. We often have the desire for revenge - a desire to get even - welling up inside us. David had that same desire, and yet he knew that it was sin to take matters into his own hands, so he prayed to the Lord and asked God to deal with those who sought to do him harm or even kill him. David makes a list of things - almost as a suggestion - as to what God can do to these people, but in reality David knows that it is only up to God to do what He chooses. David has seen what God can do to the ungodly, and draws from that experience, knowing that God will handle it the best way possible for all concerned.
Read Matthew 5:43-48 and make a list of ways to pray for those who treat you badly. Now, it's time to leave the matter in God's hands.

Saturday • Psalm 35:15-28

DIGGING DEEPER • We have seen times when people are glad that bad things happen to others. Some even cheer and rejoice when a person is in trouble or is going through hard times. Deceitful people sometimes make up lies to make us look bad and try to get our friends to turn against us. David called on the name of the Lord to right this wrong by asking the Lord to vindicate him, and to let those who lied about him be brought to mutual confusion and clothed in shame and dishonor. This request may seem harsh, but David is leaving it in the Lord's hands and is interested in righting a wrong so that all others would know the truth.
Ask the Lord to bring to mind a time when someone lied about you. How did you feel? Now, ask the Lord to remind you if you have done the same to anyone else. If you have, be sure to go and correct the situation.

qt WEEK 3

Every day we see the struggle between good and evil in the world. People make a great effort in hopes that somehow their life really can be better. This week we will see that the only way that will happen is if we trust in the Lord, call on Him, and rest in His strength as we seek to live a righteous life.

Prayer focus for this week

Q: The Question — *What is the writer saying?*
A: The Answer — *How Can I apply this to my life?*

Sunday • Psalm 36:1-12

Never figure out
Vast like Mountains

DIGGING DEEPER • There are some friends we have grown up with whom we know quite well. How disappointing it can be to learn something unpleasant about their past, the way they think about an issue, or even their personality. David lays out the difference between what the ungodly know of God and what the righteous know of Him. He starts out in verse 1 with a negative description of the wicked, who have "no fear of God" (fear in this verse means the proper regard for a sinner facing a righteous and divine judge). His words are wickedness and deceit; he has ceased to be wise and no longer does good. The wicked have fallen and have been cast down, unable to rise again. In contrast, the righteous know God's mercy, faithfulness, righteousness, and lovingkindness.
List what aspects of righteousness can be known of God from verses 5-10.

Monday • Psalm 37:1-13

Q/A: *Trust in God, no matter what. He's got your back. Commit yourself to the Lord.*

DIGGING DEEPER • Remember the sound advice you've received over the years? – Look both ways before crossing the street; don't talk to strangers; never stick your tongue onto a steel post in winter (Ouch!). David also offers words to live by as he tells his readers to "Fret not thyself because of evildoers…Trust in the LORD, and do good…Delight thyself also in the Lord…Commit thy way unto the LORD…Rest in the LORD, and wait patiently for him…Cease from anger, and forsake wrath: fret not thyself in any wise to do evil." These are some of the ways in which the righteous can grow to spiritual maturity.
Write a short letter to someone you know who would be encouraged by the advice in this Psalm, using only the points that would apply to them.

Tuesday • Psalm 37:14-26

Q/A: *Again…Trust God. Do something you normally wouldn't do and see how God works.*

DIGGING DEEPER • Psalm 37 has much to say about the wicked and the righteous. The principle person of the Psalm is the Lord, who is named over a dozen times. He knows exactly what is happening every day in the lives of the upright. At the same time, He keeps His eye on the wicked and foresees their judgment. In the words of the psalmist, He upholds the righteous and will cut off the wicked. If the righteous (believers) will rest upon that assurance, they will be blessed in many ways and that blessing will be passed on to their descendents. We get to choose whether we are named among the wicked or the righteous, but God decides the outcome of our choices. Remember, good choices will positively affect future generations.
Ask your club leader for a Christian Service you can do for someone in your church that will encourage him to trust the Lord more fully.

Wednesday • Psalm 37:27-40

- Will not forsake his faithful ones
- offspring of the wicked will be cut off
- His feet do not slip
- The wicked lie in wait for righteous
- All sinners will be destroyed
- future of the wicked will be cut off.

DIGGING DEEPER • Many of us have attended the funeral of a friend who is still a teenager, or know someone who has died unexpectedly at a very young age. Have you ever thought, "Where are they spending eternity?" There is more to life than just our time here on earth. The psalmist wants us to gain an eternal perspective that will cause us to "Depart from evil, and do good." The time will surely come when the wicked will no longer be on earth or in heaven. Their apparent prosperity is temporary, but the righteous are forever. How does one learn to live day to day with eternity's values in view? The answer is in the last three words of the Psalm: "Trust in him" (in the salvation that is of the Lord).
List five characteristics of the righteous and five of the ungodly from this Psalm. Which do you want to be characteristic of your life?

Thursday • Psalm 38:1-11

Confess your sins to God

DIGGING DEEPER • Sin brings displeasure to the Lord. To the sinner, it brings the following: conviction, restlessness, burdensomeness, corruption, trouble, shame, mourning, sickness, feebleness, brokenness, groaning, weakness, and loneliness. Whew, that's quite a list of negatives! Such is the terrible price for a moment's lustful gratification. God has preserved this record for our benefit. Although David confessed and received forgiveness, he still had to face the dire consequences of his sin. He was so overcome by guilt, shame, and remorse that it took many months before he could attain complete healing and appropriate the blessedness of forgiveness.
Read 1 John 1:9 and bring all your unconfessed sins before the Lord so that He may cleanse and forgive you.

Friday • Psalm 38:12-22

Give your day to God. He can help you with your problems.

DIGGING DEEPER • There are times when we just do not have the strength to face the day and the problems it presents. Sometimes we come up against our enemies, including Satan, and find that we are no match. David confesses his inability to cope with the enemy. He confesses his current condition and repeats his confession of guilt and repentance. He also expresses the reasons why a just God should come to his aid. His enemies are strong and confident of their ability to carry out their threats, but David is confident that God is stronger than they. He ends the Psalm with a very passionate plea to God. He realizes that God is his best and only real help – someone who is ready and willing to come to his aid.
Take a minute and list three things you do not have the energy, capability, or strength to accomplish, then ask God to help you overcome them.

Saturday • Psalm 39:1-13

Willingness to serve humbly
Easiness to forgive

DIGGING DEEPER • Today many people want to know the future. They read their horoscopes and consult mediums and fortune tellers, so they can get a little glimpse of what the future may hold. David acknowledges that it is futile for anyone to attempt to program his own future, because God is in control of the length of our lives. But interestingly enough, he still asked the Lord to let him know what the future held for him. While he was voicing his request, he suddenly was struck dumb by the thought that God Himself was permitting the hardships in his life! God was buffeting him because of iniquity in his life. Actually, the Lord was molding him into " a vessel unto honour, sanctified, and meet (fit) for the master's use, and prepared unto every good work" (2 Timothy 2:21).
List two things the Lord has used to mold and make you useful for Him.

qt WEEK 4

Our lives are filled with experiences from the awesome to the awful. We go from great joy and happiness to deep discouragement in moments. God is always our rock and our foundation, our hope and light. Christ knew that of His Heavenly Father when He faced the cross. We also need to know that as we live our lives.

Prayer focus for this week

Q: The Question *What is the writer saying?*
A: The Answer *How Can I apply this to my life?*

Sunday • Psalm 40:1-17

Sometimes the bad or hard times in life make us stronger. It helps us to relay on God instead of ourselves.

DIGGING DEEPER • As is the case in several other messianic Psalms, some portions speak of Christ, some of the psalmist, and some of both. David's horrible pit experience came when he was consumed by remorse after his sin with Bathsheba (Psalm 38:3-8). His new song came when he appropriated the blessedness of forgiveness. Jesus' pit experience occurred on Calvary when, burdened with our sins, His soul suffered anguish beyond understanding (Psalm 22:1) and His body was subjected to agony above measure (Psalm 22:15). His new song came in His resurrection (Psalm 22:22; Hebrews 2:12). We may have similar experiences of hope and rejoicing as did David and our Lord.
Take time in prayer to thank the Lord for deliverance from the horrible pit times of life. They won't last forever!

Monday • Psalm 41:1-13

Q Forgiving others easily
A

DIGGING DEEPER • In considering Psalm 41 as one of the messianic Psalms, verse 9 focuses on the night of Jesus' betrayal by Judas (John 13:18-19). He wanted the disciples to know that the events which would soon overwhelm them were all foreseen by Him. Historically, the "familiar (close) friend" in David's life was Ahithophel (2 Samuel 15:12; 16:23). He was Bathsheba's grandfather (2 Samuel 11:3; 23:34), and has some interesting comparisons to Judas Iscariot. He was a close friend, bargained with the enemy, asked for a band of men, and ended his life by hanging himself (2 Samuel 17:23). Just as God's grace was enough for David and Jesus, it is all we will need for our daily lives, regardless of what we face.
List two things that God's grace has helped you deal with in your life. How can you help others realize the same thing about grace?

Tuesday • Psalm 42:1-11

Q
A

DIGGING DEEPER • We have heard stories of people being lost in the forest, on a mountain, or at sea. Many people give up and die because they lose hope of ever being found, but those who survive tell a similar story of the hope they had of being found. The psalmist longs for God because of his sorrow day and night. He asks a rhetorical question in verse 5, then in turn offers a solution: "Why art thou cast down, O my soul? ...hope thou in God." When our soul is cast down or discouraged and depressed, it is to our advantage to remember the Lord, His lovingkindness, and that He is our rock.
State the reasons you have hope in God, and how you can encourage your friends with how He has helped you. Name two friends who need to hear of your hope in God.

Wednesday • Psalm 43:1-5

DIGGING DEEPER • At one time or another, most of us have prayed that the Lord would help us get out of a bad situation, whether it was at school, with our parents, or with our enemies. That prayer is not always answered the way we like, but the Lord does give us all we need to get us through our circumstances and still bring honor to His name. Verse 2 indicates that even when it seems God has forgotten us, He is still our strength, hope, and rock. When we go outside in the dark, God doesn't suddenly turn the darkness to daytime; instead, we use a flashlight or a torch so we can see in the darkness. The psalmist asks for the light (understanding) of God's Truth to lead him through the trials of life and enable him to hope in Him.
Read Psalm 23 again and list what God did for David as he walked through the valley of his life.

Thursday • Psalm 44:1-14

DIGGING DEEPER • Do you ever find yourself believing that you have to do everything yourself if you want to be successful? Is it hard for you to ask for help, or to say thank you when someone lends you a hand? Do you believe sometimes that God is really quite fortunate to have you serving Him? The reality is that without Him we can do nothing and we are nothing. The psalmist admits that the reason Israel was successful when they defeated their enemies was that God drove out the nations by His hand, and it was His right hand that gave them the land, not their own sword. Only when they did not follow after God and were disobedient did God use their enemies to punish them.
Compare 1 Corinthians 11:23-31 with today's passage to see how God treats rebellion and unconfessed sin. What should you do about it?

Friday • Psalm 44:15-26

DIGGING DEEPER • "Not Fair!" These are familiar words to all of us when we or our friends feel we are getting a bad break or a raw deal. We believe that we deserve something better and we are going to tell everyone about it. The psalmist believes the same thing. He doesn't believe that he or Israel deserves such treatment by God. They are confused as to why God doesn't consider the fact that they haven't turned from Him and gone after foreign gods. Why hasn't He brought relief from their enemy? He even accuses God of being asleep. The reality is that we all deserve hell, and everything outside of that is just God's mercy to us. God does hear our cry for help and understands even if we question Him.
List six blessings you don't deserve and then thank Him for each of them. Now go and tell someone today of at least one of them.

Saturday • Psalm 45:1-17

DIGGING DEEPER • There are seven divisions in this Psalm depicting the establishment of the future reign of Christ on earth (Daniel 2:44):
1. The King's majestic beauty and graciousness – He's lovely and gracious.
2. The King's arrival in might, glory, and majesty – He appears in great majesty.
3. The deity of the King and His authority – He is the rightful ruler.
4. The marriage of the King – He is prepared to accept us as His bride.
5. The bride's submission to the King – We gladly love and obey Him.
6. The bride's associates and the wedding guests – All are made welcome.
7. The worldwide and eternal praise of the King – All shall praise Him.
There will come a day when Christ will rule on this earth and all his children with Him. Those who don't belong to Christ will be judged and sent to hell.

qt WEEK 5

When someone drives a car, he learns to look in all directions to see what is going on around him. In our Christian lives we need to understand Who our God is, who we are in Christ, and all that we have through Him. Our lives should reflect that we know God, trust Him, and honor Him with our whole heart.

Prayer focus for this week

Q: The Question — *What is the writer saying?*
A: The Answer — *How Can I apply this to my life?*

Sunday • Psalm 46:1-11

DIGGING DEEPER • Little children often believe that their father can do anything and that he is stronger than anyone, even the biggest bear in the woods. In many cases, no matter what the danger may be, there is safety in the arms of our dad. Today the psalmist states the fact that his Heavenly Father truly can do everything and really is mightier than any nation, king, or kingdom. We have no fear because God is our refuge, strength, and help even if the earth is greatly altered by earthquakes, floods, even tsunamis. Today's headline news is filled with comments from arrogant leaders and nations who do not trust in God. It was the same in Korah's day (the author of this Psalm) when he wrote, "The heathen raged, the kingdoms were moved: he uttered his voice, the earth melted."
List two things for which you have yet to trust the Lord. Trust Him today.

Monday • Psalm 47:1-9

Q
A

DIGGING DEEPER • Around the world there are celebrations when a winning team comes home from a victory, especially if it's an international sport. Usually there is a parade and recognition from city officials while people come out to cheer and rejoice together over the victory of their team. Psalm 47 describes a celebration in recognition of Who God is and what He has done for His people. He is awesome, and the great King over all the earth. God has gone out with a shout. Just imagine the Creator of the universe shouting–won't that be great! He reigns over the nations and sits on His holy throne, and He has chosen our inheritance for us. This is true of the nation of Israel and for every believer. Our inheritance is heaven, and that's something for which to rejoice!
List two things for which you can rejoice; then share it with two others.

Tuesday • Psalm 48:1-14

Q
A

DIGGING DEEPER • Most of us have a favorite place that we like to visit or talk about with our friends. The psalmist's favorite spot was the city of Jerusalem, because it is the city of God. When he refers to the sides of the north, he's talking about God's heavenly dwelling place. It's difficult to adequately describe this place, as Paul readily admits (2 Corinthians 12:1-4). The idea in Psalm 48 is that God has brought His dwelling place down to earth. Verse 14 is the natural response of someone who understands the significance of the city of God and His purposes. "For this God is our God for ever and ever: he will be our guide even unto death." This is a great verse for a couple that is dating or for newlyweds!
List three ways in which God guides us. Is there an area in your life that is still under construction? Allow the Lord to complete His plan in your life.

Wednesday • Psalm 49:1-11

DIGGING DEEPER • If we were to read in the news that a person drowned because he wouldn't let go of a money bag or some important item he possessed, we would think him a fool, but that is what people do every day when they put their trust in riches above their love for God. The message in this passage is just as important today as it was in the psalmist's day or in the day when Jesus spoke the parable of Luke 12:15-21: "Life consisteth not in the abundance of things which he possesseth." The key verse in today's passage is verse 7: "None of them (who trust in their wealth) can by any means redeem his brother, nor give to God a ransom for him." Life is more important than riches, so live like we believe it.
Read Luke 12:15-21 and list two problems the rich man had and two observations Christ makes that would help the rich solve that problem.

Thursday • Psalm 49:12-20

DIGGING DEEPER • We all know of rich and famous people who have died. We have possibly seen pictures of the actual funeral services on TV. No matter how rich or popular, one thing is the same; they leave it all behind. There are no trailers or suitcases attached to a hearse. In today's passage we are reminded that we should not put great emphasis on riches or power, but on the fact that our soul is redeemed by God. Trusting in riches is a poor investment when it comes to eternity. A person of honor dies and decays just like everyone else. The important thing is whether or not one has a saving knowledge of the Lord Jesus Christ and the redemption He offers.
Have you put your trust in Christ for your salvation? Are you redeemed from your sin? Whom have you told about Christ this month?

Friday • Psalm 50:1-13

DIGGING DEEPER • Sometimes the traditions we observe prevent us from benefiting from what is truly important. God reproves Israel for having wrong motives in offering their animal sacrifices. He is not objecting to the procedures being used, but to their reasoning. Their thinking is like that of the surrounding heathen worshipers - that God is dependent on them for His food and He should be grateful. How perverted! They miss the whole point of a holy and merciful God devising a means by which He is able to have intimate communion with a sinful people. Their sacrifices should be a sign of gratefulness, recognizing their sinfulness as contrasted to God's holiness. Perverted worship is a shocking sin against God. **When you go to church, do you concentrate on your worship of God or on the people who are there and the activities going on around you?**

Saturday • Psalm 50:14-23

DIGGING DEEPER • When we get a job, we are to do what the boss tells us. It's a way of showing our appreciation for hiring us as well as a good testimony of our diligence. The psalmist gives us instructions for showing our appreciation to God for redeeming us. We begin with offering thanksgiving. Thanksgiving is preventative maintenance for the sins of covetousness, envy, and greed. Next, we need to be careful to pay any vow made unto the Lord. We end with learning to call upon the Lord. This is a remedy for egotistical pride and self-reliance. God's continual complaint against His people was their failure to call upon Him. The psalmist delighted in observing these requests by God in Psalm 116:16-18. **What a blessing to be a part of God's family and program. We should live up to God's expectations because we love and honor him.**

qt WEEK 6

Are you ready for an extreme makeover? We all have our ideas about how we would look, but God has His own plans for us. At the end of this week's quiet time, the new you will be revealed! Who will you look like after God does an extreme makeover on you?

Prayer focus for this week

Q: The Question *What is the writer saying?*
A: The Answer *How Can I apply this to my life?*

Sunday • 2 Corinthians 1:1-11

DIGGING DEEPER • "Why are you doing this to me, God?" If you have not asked God this question yet, you probably will. Today we start the book of 2 Corinthians in our quiet time. Paul knew a lot about trouble (Acts 19:23-20:3), and he knew that God always had a purpose in it. God comforts us so that we can comfort others (v. 4). Notice in verse 6 that whenever we have trouble it comes about so we can encourage someone else who is having trouble. There's a saying, "God never wastes a hurt." God brings you through the trouble you are having. You will soon discover others who are having trouble, too, so you can be an encouragement to them. **Has God already delivered you from trouble? How did He do it? Look for someone today that has trouble. Encourage him today just as God has encouraged you.**

Monday • 2 Corinthians 1:12-24

DIGGING DEEPER • Have you ever been falsely accused? Paul had written the book of 1 Corinthians to the church in Corinth one year before. Now he writes his follow-up letter. Paul talks about his conscience being honest before the people (v. 12). He had rebuked the church for sin that was allowed to continue; now he is sharing his love for them (v. 14). Paul had to defend his truthfulness in verses 15-20 by saying that he was truthful, just as all the promises of God would be fulfilled in Jesus Christ. Paul was honest before God the Father, Son, and Holy Spirit (vv. 21-24) and viewed himself as a fellow helper to the Corinthian believers.
What do you think Paul thought about God? What do you think he thought about himself? What do you think he thought about other people? How would you answer these questions about yourself?

Tuesday • 2 Corinthians 2:1-13

DIGGING DEEPER • False teachers had lied about Paul to the church in Corinth. Now Paul tells the church why he had not come back to see them. His love for them caused him to stay away so that they would have a chance to correct the sin in the church. It was love that motivated Paul (vv. 1-4). In verses 5-11, Paul tells them to forgive the man who had sinned (1 Corinthians 5) and to restore him into fellowship. Once a person asks God and fellow Christians for forgiveness, we have to forgive that person. Paul is also showing his need for Christian fellowship (vv. 12-13). He needed the encouragement of Titus, and he went looking for him.
Have you forgiven someone who has sinned against you? How many reasons for forgiveness can you find in today's verses?

Wednesday • 2 Corinthians 2:14 - 3:5

DIGGING DEEPER • Paul is discouraged, but in his discouragement he sees himself in a great triumphant procession (v. 14). Jesus Christ is the Great General who is leading Paul. Paul is following God and he is telling the truth to lost and saved people (vv. 15-17). People are important to Paul (vv. 1-5). What these people were in Christ was the proof of Paul's ministry. Those people had been changed and their lives were proof that Paul was teaching the truth. It was not Paul who was adequate within himself, but Christ made him adequate to do God's will. (Compare 2:16 with 3:5.)

Are you discouraged today? Ask God to allow you to view yourself in the great victory procession Paul describes here. Do you feel you cannot succeed in the Christian life? Be sure you are trusting in God alone today.

Thursday • 2 Corinthians 3:6-18

DIGGING DEEPER • Do you understand the New Testament (v. 6) and the Old Testament (v. 14)? Paul tells us that the Old Testament Law only brought death. The New Testament (new covenant) brought life. The false teachers in Corinth were teaching legalism. They wanted people to live by a list of rules. The new covenant is based on living life in the power of the Holy Spirit and becoming just like Jesus Christ. Paul had become a minister of the new covenant; he was living his life in the power and liberty found in Jesus Christ.

Are you becoming more and more like Jesus every day (v. 18)? Do you live your life by rules, or are you allowing the Holy Spirit and the Word of God to transform you into the person that God wants you to be?

Friday • 2 Corinthians 4:1-7

DIGGING DEEPER • Every Christian is called into ministry. Paul's special ministry always amazed him. He never got over the fact that he had received mercy from God. It kept him going all the time. Every Christian who ministers must live a pure life and have a clear conscience. We are just servants preaching and teaching Jesus Christ to people who are lost and blind. God has shined His light into our hearts and it is His light, His glory in us that is truly amazing. Paul says that we are just clay pots (v. 7) and the real treasure inside us is Jesus Christ and His Gospel. No one really notices the clay pot when Jesus is shining out.
What are you doing this week to let the light of the Gospel shine out of your life to others? How do you resemble a clay pot? How would you describe the glory and life of Jesus Christ?

Saturday • 2 Corinthians 4:8-18

DIGGING DEEPER • We all like to be happy as we serve the Lord. Paul has spent a lot of time in the previous verses talking about the glory of God (4:6) and how we are changed into looking just like Jesus from glory to glory (3:18). Now, Paul tells us that suffering for Jesus Christ is a big part of bringing glory to God. One of the keys to understanding why God allows trouble in our lives is found in verse 11: that the life also of Jesus might be made manifest (revealed) in our mortal flesh. Paul tells us to look on the things that are eternal. There is more to life than just what happens to us on the outside.
List the trouble that you have today. Now list what God has done for you already through salvation, and what He will do for you throughout all eternity. Can you see how God is using you for His glory?

qt WEEK 7

Who is your hero? Whom do you want to be like? Paul wanted to be just like Jesus, and because of that, we should be happy to follow Paul as he followed Christ. Paul's genuine love for Christ and others is revealed in this week's quiet time.

Prayer focus for this week

Q: The Question *What is the writer saying?*
A: The Answer *How Can I apply this to my life?*

Sunday • 2 Corinthians 5:1-10

DIGGING DEEPER • Do you ever wonder what will happen to you when you die? Paul was not afraid to die. In fact, he really wanted to be in Heaven with the Lord. Paul had complete confidence in God that, at the very moment he was absent from the body (when he died), he would be present with the Lord! Paul had a godly ambition also. Verse 9 speaks of having as our ambition …to be pleasing to Him. This is the noblest of all ambitions! Paul lived each moment knowing that we all would one day appear before the judgment seat of Christ.

Ask God today to make Heaven as real to you as it was to Paul! Is your greatest ambition to please Christ? Are you living today with the Judgment Seat of Christ in mind?

Monday • 2 Corinthians 5:11-21

DIGGING DEEPER • What is your greatest ambition? Paul already told us that his greatest ambition was to please Christ (v. 9). Now, Paul pours on the reasons for serving Christ. The terror of the Lord (v. 11), knowing that God would judge the Christian, was a motivation. The love of Christ motivated Paul in verse 14. He knew that God had given him the ministry of reconciliation and the word of reconciliation (vv. 18-19). Paul knew that he was an ambassador for Christ, and his job was to urge men to come to God. Because Jesus took our sin upon Himself, we are made righteous before God.
Can you see that God has called you to be an ambassador just like He called Paul? Will you tell someone about how he or she can be reconciled to God today? Will you let the love of Christ motivate you today?

Tuesday • 2 Corinthians 6:1-10

DIGGING DEEPER • Has anyone ever given you a job to do and instructions on how to do it? Some-times instructions just involve doing as you are told, and sometimes they get very specific. Some instructions sound like fun but often they do not describe the dirty work involved. Paul gives us a summary of his instructions in these verses today. He describes his job as working together with God. He was to urge men to be saved. He was not to offend others. He had to approve himself as a minister of God in over twenty areas. Circle the words in, by, and as to see these areas.
Are you ready for instructions that matter? List the areas in which you would have difficulty following God's instructions. What would you love to do, if you could? What will you do?

Wednesday • 2 Corinthians 6:11-7:1

DIGGING DEEPER • When love (5:14) is your motivation, then separation becomes natural. When you have a wife or a husband, you become separate from every other person on the planet in order to love your spouse exclusively. Paul's great love for Christ caused him to be separated from everything that was contrary to the mind of God (vv. 11-16a). Then Paul concluded that he was to be separated to God Himself (vv. 16b-7:1). Because of Paul's love for Christ, he couldn't think of doing anything to compromise his deep love for Him.
Are you having trouble giving up some relationship or habit that is contrary to the heart and mind of God? Will you resolve today to love God Himself above anything on earth? What are you willing to give up to enjoy unbroken fellowship with Jesus Christ?

Thursday • 2 Corinthians 7:2-16

DIGGING DEEPER • Are you a real person? Paul demonstrates his true heart of love for the Corinthians in this passage. He says, "...ye are in our hearts." He admits being fearful and depressed. He tells them that he needed people (Titus) to encourage him. Paul was rejoicing that the Corinthians had repented of their sins after his first letter and they had gone on to live out their faith with great zeal. He concludes by saying that he has confidence in them in all things. Every person needs to be loved and every person wants to be valued for who he or she is.
Is there someone in your life today that needs to hear the words "I love you" from your lips? Who needs to hear the words "I am proud of you" from you today? When we love people and value them, we should tell them, just like Paul did.

Friday • 2 Corinthians 8:1-15

DIGGING DEEPER • When you are in love, sometimes you do things that seem silly. Giving gifts to the one you love can sometimes get out of hand, but this is the nature of love. Love gives, and John 3:16 proves that point when it tells us that "...God so loved the world that he gave..." Our giving in the church is no different. Paul tells about the Macedonians who first gave themselves to the Lord and then graciously and joyously insisted on giving an offering to the Lord Jesus Christ (v. 8)! This is the greatest example of giving. Look how the words of love, faith, sincerity, joy, willingness, and grace characterized their giving.
Have you become joyful and gracious in your giving? How can the example of Christ giving His life for us motivate us to be faithful in our tithes and offerings? Can you trust God with your money?

Saturday • 2 Corinthians 8:16-24

DIGGING DEEPER • Do you know a person of integrity that you want to please? Paul was handling the generous offering of the Corinthians with absolute integrity. Because of their deep love for Christ and Paul, the offering would be large, and so Paul sent Titus and "the brother" (v. 18) who was not named. This brother and Titus were messengers of the churches, and the glory of Christ (v. 23), so you know they could be trusted. Any offering in the church given for the Lord's work should be handled in an honest way. Now it was time to give the offering that was promised. The church could have complete confidence that it would be used properly.
Have you made a promise on which you need to follow through? Are you handling your money in a way that is honoring to God?

WEEK 8

Great warriors and great athletes often must put it all on the line as they are approaching the finish line. At that point, what they have done in training and what they truly are makes the difference in winning and losing. Watch the great warrior and athlete, the Apostle Paul, win in your quiet time this week!

Prayer focus for this week

Q: The Question — *What is the writer saying?*
A: The Answer — *How Can I apply this to my life?*

Sunday • 2 Corinthians 9:1-15

DIGGING DEEPER • Have you ever heard the question "What would you do if you knew you could not fail?" Paul gives us a promise regarding giving in chapter 9 that is fail-proof. He tells us that we should always be ready to give (vv. 1-5). We should give generously (vv. 6-11a) because God is able to give you more than you ever give to Him. Then look at verse 7 and see how we should give cheerfully, because God loves a cheerful giver! God has promised to pour out His love on the person who gives cheerfully. Finally, see how thankfulness is always a part of Christian giving (vv. 11b-15) and the greatest gift of all is Jesus Christ! He is God's unspeakable gift and He is the reason that we can be cheerful givers!
Are you a cheerful giver? Have you taken God up on His promise that He is able to make all grace abound toward you?

Monday • 2 Corinthians 10:1-18

DIGGING DEEPER • Paul is on a rescue mission to save the Christians at Corinth from false teachers who are trying to discredit Paul's ministry. Verses 4-5 should be memorized by every Christian who wants to win spiritual battles. Paul knows that spiritual battles are fought in the mind and will be won with the Word of God. Paul is ready to fight false doctrine and win back the church he helped establish. Paul is a real man of God and has the credentials to prove it.
What are you ready to fight for? Paul loved God, people, and the truth of God's Word. Check your life and see what you are willing to fight to defend.

Tuesday • 2 Corinthians 11:1-15

DIGGING DEEPER • Paul loves his converts at Corinth, but Satan has come into the church and is trying to steal the bride of Christ out of it. The super apostles or false teachers who have come into the church (v. 4) are teaching another Jesus, are led by a false spirit, and are teaching a different gospel. Paul declares his love (v. 11) and warns them that these false apostles (vv. 13-15) look like the real thing, but in fact are following Satan and will ultimately be destroyed.
To whom are you listening, and what are you reading? Do your favorite Christian authors pass the test of Scripture? What are they teaching about Jesus Christ, the Holy Spirit, and the Gospel?

Wednesday • 2 Corinthians 11:16-33

Q&A

DIGGING DEEPER • We all know about Hollywood actors. On the screen they play the part of a different person, but in real life they are just themselves. Paul is no actor, but is a real apostle and he lists what he has done in real life to prove it. The false apostles that Paul is fighting are the actors. Look at Paul's resume of suffering. Hardly anyone could rival what Paul went through for the Gospel, for Jesus, and for the Christians to whom he ministered. Listen to Paul share his heartfelt love for the Corinthian believers. Paul's steadfastness in the face of extreme adversity should encourage every Christian to keep on keeping on for Jesus!

Are you afraid to suffer for Jesus Christ? What will it take for you to turn back from serving Christ and others? Why not write out your commitment to Christ, telling Him that you are willing to follow Him no matter the cost?

Thursday • 2 Corinthians 12:1-10

Q&A

DIGGING DEEPER • If you go to certain areas of the Pentagon, you must have security clearance in order to hear the greatest secrets of our government. Paul was granted top security clearance by God and ushered into the third Heaven where he heard unspeakable words. He is talking about how God inspired him to write Scripture. Because of this great privilege, God also gave him a thorn in the flesh, apparently some physical sickness or affliction, to be sure he always remained humble. Paul's "thorn" was not removed, but God gave him the grace to glory in it so he could have the power of God on his life.

How are you viewing your various troubles (v. 10)? If God refuses to remove them, He will give you grace to live with them for His Glory. What are you willing to live with in order to have God's power in your life?

Friday • 2 Corinthians 12:11-21

DIGGING DEEPER • Whom can you trust in life? Paul tells us that he is trustworthy and his life and credentials as an apostle cannot be disputed. Comparing Scripture with Scripture throughout the New Testament, we see the uniqueness of the office of apostle that Paul fulfilled. Now that the canon of Scripture is complete, the office is no longer in existence. Finally, Paul uses strong warnings to the church, based on his apostles' office (v. 11), his love for them (v. 15), and his desire to build them up (v. 19). He challenges them to clean up the sin that has been allowed to run through the church.

Whom can you encourage (edify) in their walk with Christ this week? Be sure to make an appointment to talk with them, heart to heart, about the things that matter most to God.

Saturday • 2 Corinthians 13:1-14

DIGGING DEEPER • Everyone who goes to school eventually has to take a test. Paul has finished his second letter to the Corinthians. He has been a faithful teacher; he has the proper balance of love and sternness. They know he has taught them the truth. Now they must take the test to see if they are true Christians. Examine yourselves whether you be in the faith, he says. He wants them to look into their hearts and see that they really are true believers in Christ. Paul wants them to be assured of their salvation and be perfect (mature) in their walk with Christ.

What about you? When you examine yourself, do you find that you are a true believer? Have you repented of your sin and put your complete trust in Christ alone for your salvation? How will your life be changed after your study of 2 Corinthians?

qt WEEK 9

Are you excited to begin a study of Genesis? In Genesis you'll find all the beginnings of everything as well as setting the stage for God's unfolding plan of redemption. Get ready for some exciting firsts this week looking at Adam and Eve and several of their descendants.

Prayer focus for this week

Q: The Question — *What is the writer saying?*
A: The Answer — *How Can I apply this to my life?*

Sunday • Genesis 1:1-19

DIGGING DEEPER • Do you believe the Biblical account about the origin of the world in which we live? Notice that God doesn't begin His story of creation with Day 1, but with explaining who He, as the Creator, was. How did God create? He used His power and wisdom (Jeremiah 10:12) and His Word (Psalm 33:6-9). Why did He create? To bring glory to Himself (Psalm 19:1-3), and for His own pleasure (Revelation 4:11). Each day in Genesis is one rotation of the Earth upon its axis–a 24-hour period (Exodus 20:11). Did you notice that God didn't create the sun, moon, and stars until the fourth day? God didn't need them because He is light (1 John 1:5) and He dwells in light (1 Timothy 6:16). He created them to help us!
Look at the world around you and think about which is easier to believe: Did God create everything, or did it all just happen by accident?

Monday • Genesis 1:20-2:3

Q&A

DIGGING DEEPER • Why are we here? God created us in His image to reflect His traits and qualities such as love, truth, wisdom, holiness, justice, creativity, and many more. From Genesis to Revelation, the Bible recognizes three heavens. The first is where the birds fly (Jeremiah 4:25) and where the clouds are (Deuteronomy 11:11). The second heaven is where the sun, moon, and stars shine (Genesis 15:5). The third heaven is where the throne of God is located (Isaiah 66:1; Matthew 5:34). God didn't rest on the seventh day because He was tired. He gloried in His great work which had been completed for His pleasure.
Upon which of God's traits and qualities can you reflect today? Think about God as the Creator and about all He has provided for us. Praise Him for it!

Tuesday • Genesis 2:4-25

Q&A

DIGGING DEEPER • Why is the creation story retold here? Chapter 1 gives an overview of all creation, while chapter 2 focuses on man. In telling how He brought man and his environment into being, God chose to use three different verbs translated created, made, and formed. This indicates God used at least three different types of activity in the process of creation. This Genesis account, together with the New Testament, teaches that God intends for marriage to be monogamous, heterosexual, and permanent (Mark 10:6-9). The marriage union is to be a picture of the relationship between Christ and His church (Ephesians 5:22-33).
Think about all of creation and the three words God used to describe and create it. What can you do to determine that your (future) marriage will be a picture of Christ and the church?

Wednesday • Genesis 3:1-19

Q&A

DIGGING DEEPER • Have you ever been tempted to say that the devil made you do something? He can't make you do anything! Satan has many tools he uses to tempt us to disobey God's commands. Eve was tempted by the lust of the flesh, the lust of the eyes, and the pride of life (1 John 2:16). Jesus Christ is the seed of the woman. His death on the cross seemed to be a victory for Satan; however, as a result of His death on the cross, Jesus now has the church as His body on the Earth. With the feet of that body He will crush Satan. In Adam we inherited a curse, sweat, and death. In Christ we can receive blessing, rest, and life.
Are you in Adam or in Christ? Ask Jesus to help you learn to recognize Satan's tools of temptation. Determine how you are going to resist them the next time you are tempted.

Thursday • Genesis 3:20-4:12

Q&A

DIGGING DEEPER • Do you want to be righteous or sinful? Righteous, of course! Throughout Scripture, to be clothed is to be righteous in the eyes of God, and to be naked is to be sinful. Adam and Eve's attempt to cover their sin was inadequate. God provided for their nakedness but it cost the life of an innocent animal. Abel typifies Christ in that he was a shepherd who offered an acceptable sacrifice to God. Cain typifies a religious man who tries to choose his own worship and rejects redemption by blood. There is more to Genesis than the passages that have been selected here as most helpful for our study. Please find the time to read all of Genesis during this study.
Would others say you were righteous or sinful? Are you trying to cover your own sin? Trust Jesus' provision for your sin.

Friday • Genesis 4:25-5:14

DIGGING DEEPER • Can you imagine what it would be like to live for nine hundred years? If you were born in A.D. 1107, you'd still have about one hundred years left to go. You would have seen and experienced a lot! Through Seth, God established a line which would call upon the name of the LORD. This line includes Noah, Abraham, Isaac, and Jacob. This is the line from which the Lord would bring Jesus Christ to redeem His own from the curse of Adam's sin. The book of Genesis is largely an account of the Lord's dealings with this line for more than twenty generations. Sin brought immediate spiritual death to Adam. As his descendants we inherited that death, but God provided a way to bring life out of that death.
Do you have that life? If you do, praise God and ask your friends to make sure they have it as well. If not, ask someone to help you receive it.

Saturday • Genesis 5:15-32

DIGGING DEEPER • Can you imagine what it would be like to know your fifth-great-grandpa? Enoch did! Enoch was 308 years old when Adam died and was translated (taken) to be with God fifty five years before Seth died. Because of his faith and faithfulness, he brought assurance of life beyond the grave to those who lived before and after him. Six generations of ancestors before him and two generations of his descendants no doubt heard him preach. Look at Methuselah: at 969, he was the oldest person ever to have lived. His life spanned eleven generations! He lived for 243 years at the same time as Adam, and 100 years with the sons of Noah.
Read Romans 15:4 and 1 Corinthians 10:11 to see how Enoch's and Methuselah's lives are relevant for you today. Are you living a life as close to God as possible, as Enoch did? Do others see and hear your witness?

qt WEEK 10

Do you have God's attention? Are you willing to do what God asks of you, even if it's hard and takes a long time? This week we'll examine how Noah got God's attention, why God worked in his life to save a few people from a worldwide catastrophe, and what symbol He gave that it would never happen again.

Prayer focus for this week

Q: The Question *What is the writer saying?*
A: The Answer *How Can I apply this to my life?*

Sunday • Genesis 6:1-16

DIGGING DEEPER • Who were the "sons of God"? Examining Scripture, we find Job 1:6 and 2:1 say that angelic beings were called "sons of God." Some respected interpreters conclude that they are the angels who kept not their first estate (Jude 6), the angels that sinned (2 Peter 2:4), and possibly the spirits in prison (1 Peter 3:19). Consider the following: 1. Jesus indicated in Mark 12:25 that the angels in heaven do not marry. 2. The judgment of the flood was for the wickedness of man. Noah got God's attention by being righteous, and God warned him about what was going to come and how to prepare for it.

Who you are before God is more important than who the "sons of God" were. Does God have your attention? Noah got God's attention by his righteousness. Confess any sin to God to get started.

Monday • Genesis 6:17-7:10

DIGGING DEEPER • Do you have a problem believing all the details in the story of Noah, the ark, and the flood? Jesus believed them (Matthew 24:37-39). Were Noah and his family saved from drowning by what he did or by what he believed? If Noah had not believed what God said, he would not have built the ark and would have perished. His faith came first and produced his works, which saved his household (Hebrews 11:7). His works proved his faith (James 2:18). Note that the Lord let Noah know why he needed to build the ark. Then He told him precisely how to build it. God doesn't always tell us why and how; that's where faith comes in. Plus, we have God's written Word, through which He talks to us.
Has God asked you to do something? Believe Him and do it! Dig a little deeper in God's Word by looking up the references above.

Tuesday • Genesis 7:11-24

DIGGING DEEPER • Have you ever wondered how Noah and his family were able to feed and care for all the animals that were on the ark for such a long time? It was simple…they did all that God commanded (6:22; 7:5, 16) and God did the rest. Think about how, at a specific time, less than five thousand years ago, God intervened in the affairs of man. In a very dramatic way, He altered the natural processes which He had established almost two thousand years previously. With what God reveals in the early chapters of Genesis, together with the clarification given by later Scriptures, we have the basis for our understanding of the world around us today.
What is God commanding you to do today? Memorize Scripture? Do your Quiet Time? Witness to your friends? It can't be as hard as Noah had it.

Wednesday • Genesis 8:1-12

Q&A

DIGGING DEEPER • How big do you think the flood really was? Did it cover the whole Earth, or was it somewhat localized? The flood was worldwide! The Scriptures, the physical properties of water, and the law of gravity support a worldwide flood. How did God bring about the flood? Not only were the fountains of the deep released, but it rained unusually hard for forty days. Then, it is possible that the combination of lighter, steadier rain, and subterranean water upheavals continued for an additional 110 days. Perhaps one reason that God does not give us the complete details in His Word is that He wants us to have the joy of anticipating full discovery later. Think about how long Noah and his family were on the ark.
Think about the awesome power God has! Praise and thank Him for it. What are you anticipating to have revealed to you when you get to heaven?

Thursday • Genesis 8:13-22

Q&A

DIGGING DEEPER • Just how long were Noah and his family on the ark? By comparing Genesis 7:10-11 with 8:13-14 we are able to determine the number of days they were confined. It was just over a year! Knowing there would be many critics, God let us know precise information He had given to Noah. He followed that by giving us the exact calendar of events occurring during the year of the flood. Look at how the time before the flood was described…the earth was corrupt and full of violence. Does that sound like the world you live in? What was the first thing Noah did after departing from the ark? He built an altar, made a sacrifice, and worshipped the Lord.
How would you have done if confined to the ark for over a year? What hard thing is God asking you to do? Obey with faith, knowing God is in control.

Friday • Genesis 9:1-19

DIGGING DEEPER • Did you notice that God had some specific instructions for Noah and his sons? They were to multiply and fill the Earth and have authority over the animals, and they were able to eat meat. Also, God included the principle of capital punishment: any individual who murders for any reason is wrong. God gives the responsibility of capital punishment to governments. No one had ever seen a rainbow before. It was God's guarantee to all mankind that there will never be a worldwide flood again. There have been floods since then, but none that were worldwide. We are all descendants of Shem, Ham, or Japheth.
Thank God for keeping His promise! What other promises can you rely on? What instructions is God giving you? Read Chapter 10.

Saturday • Genesis 11:1-9

DIGGING DEEPER • Were the people following God's instructions? No; they were staying together and trying to rely on themselves instead of on God. So God arranged a way for them to go in different directions. Observe that the patriarchs listed from Adam to Noah averaged 912 years at death. The first three generations after the flood lived an average of 445 years. The first three generations after Babel lived an average of 236 years. After that time, longevity gradually decreased until it averaged seventy to eighty years. The point is that part of the judgments of God in the flood and in the confusion of languages was to cut man's life span.
Are you following God's instructions? Read Proverbs 3:6 and Jeremiah 10:23 to find out how you should make decisions about your life.

WEEK 11

What do you do when you are tested? Several people face tests this week, and there are some name changes. God asks someone to leave his homeland, then he has to rescue a relative when he's taken captive, and a great priest comes later to bless him. Through it all, God gives and keeps His promises.

Prayer focus for this week

Q: The Question — *What is the writer saying?*
A: The Answer — *How Can I apply this to my life?*

Sunday • Genesis 12:1-20

Q
A

DIGGING DEEPER • Have you ever played the game Trust, where you are blindfolded, cross your arms, and fall back, hoping your friends will catch you before you hit the floor? These verses teach us a lot about trust. The first eleven chapters of Genesis focus on God's dealings with Abram's ancestors. The remainder will focus on the Lord's dealings with him and his descendants. God asked Abram to separate himself from an idolatrous society and go to a land that He would show him. Abram trusted and obeyed, doing exactly what God told him to do. The Lord then gave him a seven-fold promise. Abram showed great faith by obeying, especially when he didn't know where the Lord was leading him.
Are you willing to go anywhere God asks you to go? God was faithful to Abram… He'll be faithful to you! What will you trust Him for today?

Monday • Genesis 13:1-18

DIGGING DEEPER • As a child, did you sing the song, "Father Abraham had many sons; many sons had Father Abraham"? At this point in his life, Abram was an old man (around eighty) married to a barren wife. He had riches and lots of animals, but no children of his own. One of his servants would have been his logical heir. As soon as Abram and Lot separated from each other, the Lord added to His covenant with Abram. First, He showed Abram the full extent of the Promised Land. Then the Lord promised to give it to his descendants, who would not be able to be counted. What did Abram do? He built an altar to the Lord and worshipped Him!
Are you a child of God? Like Abram, is there something from which you need to separate yourself to get God's blessing? Learn to worship God.

Tuesday • Genesis 14:12-24

DIGGING DEEPER • What would you do if men came and took away someone you loved? Abram's nephew, Lot, was captured and carried away in an act of war. When Abram heard about it, he rescued Lot and all those who were with him. Who was this Melchizedek who blessed Abram? He is mentioned several times in the Bible as a priest, without a father or mother, like the Son of God, and greater than Abraham. Melchizedek was either a pre-incarnate appearance of Jesus in bodily form or an historical person foreshadowing the high priestly ministry of the resurrected Lord Jesus Christ. Abram recognized that he deserved no credit for his victory and refused to receive anything from those whom he had rescued.
Would you be ready to be taken hostage? Be a blessing to someone today by providing food, drink, or something needed in God's name.

Wednesday • Genesis 15:1-18

DIGGING DEEPER • How would you respond if God talked directly to you in a vision? What if He told you something that was way beyond anything your mind could comprehend? Abram responded by offering the first recorded request in the Bible. Abram received a negative answer because he was thinking in human terms (of course), and God had something extraordinary in mind. Abram believed in the LORD; and he counted it to him for righteousness (v. 6). This verse is quoted three times in the New Testament (Romans 4:3; Galatians 3:6; and James 2:23), teaching us that the righteousness required for salvation is passed on by God as a gift to those who believe what God says.
You have a huge advantage over Abram. It's God's written Word in your hand! Do you believe God? Do you have His righteousness?

Thursday • Genesis 17:1-8;15-19

DIGGING DEEPER • Do you know what your name means? In expanding His covenant with Abram, God changed his name to Abraham, which means Father of Many. God also changed Sarai's name to Sarah, which means Princess. Besides using the name change to confirm His promise of many descendants, God gave Abraham the sign of circumcision as an outward expression of inner faith. Notice Abraham was still thinking in terms of natural possibilities rather than God's omnipotence. God brushes aside Abraham's request to accept Ishmael by announcing the name of the son He was promising.
Do you live up to your name—Christian? Does your outward self truly express your inward self? Do you try to limit God to natural possibilities or trust Him to do above what we can comprehend?

Friday • Genesis 18:1-14

DIGGING DEEPER • How does God communicate with you? We are not told exactly how the Lord communicated with Abraham before this. By the details given in this chapter, we know that God appeared in a human form, accompanied by two angels who were also in the form of men. Note that Abraham was eager to serve them with the best he had. God again made the promise of an heir, but now told Abraham when it was going to happen. When Abraham was one hundred and Sarah was ninety, God miraculously rejuvenated their bodies so that natural conception and birth could proceed as God had promised. Is anything too hard for the Lord? Examine Matthew 19:26 and Luke 1:37 to find out. He is God, of course! **One of the main ways God communicates with us today is through His Word. Spend extra time in it examining His promises to you.**

Saturday • Genesis 22:1-18

DIGGING DEEPER • It is hard for us to understand how Abraham could even begin to offer up his son, Isaac, as a sacrifice. The Lord had repeatedly told Abraham that His promises would be fulfilled through this son, Isaac. Abraham believed the Lord even to the point of believing God would raise him from the dead (Hebrews 11:19). Look at what Abraham told his servants…that he and Isaac would go sacrifice and come back. He may not have known exactly what was going to happen, but he trusted God with the outcome of what He had promised. After Abraham passed the test, the Lord reassured him about the promises He had previously given.
Your faith won't be tested in this way, but it will be tested. Will you pass? Check out 1 Peter 1:7 and Hebrews 11:6 to see how important it is.

qt WEEK 12

Do you ever have problems with people in your family? There are plenty to go around this week! A servant is sent to find someone a wife. His prayers are answered, and a girl leaves her family to go with him. A brother tricks his dad and brother. You'll also find out where the problems in the Middle East started.

Prayer focus for this week

Q: The Question — *What is the writer saying?*
A: The Answer — *How Can I apply this to my life?*

Sunday • Genesis 24:1-15

DIGGING DEEPER • How involved do you think you'll be in picking out your future mate? Isaac was forty when Abraham sent his top servant to his homeland to get a wife for his son, with specific instructions on what to do. The servant had no plan of his own. He was sent by the father, in the name of the son, and only spoke and did as he was instructed. All of Abraham's wealth was at his disposal, and he chose what to take. Notice how specific his prayer was and how unlikely it was from a human standpoint to be answered. He wanted a young lady with a water pitcher to offer to draw water from a well for him and ten thirsty camels after a long journey. **Do you pray specific prayers like this servant did? Try it today and see how God answers. Remember that God wants the glory and He wants you to be in agreement with His purposes.**

Monday • Genesis 24:16-33

Q
A

DIGGING DEEPER • When you are faithful in doing what the Lord asks you to do and He blesses you for it, do you remember to give Him praise and thanks? That's what this servant did. The fact that Rebekah said the exact words that he had asked the Lord to put in her mouth proved that God was directing the journey. The servant praised the Lord in front of all those present, which probably impressed Rebekah as much as did the lavish gifts. Abraham lived hundreds of miles and several days journey away, but had some communication with his family, knowing there would be suitable young ladies available. Rebekah was not from a poor family, but the ten camels and jewelry were gifts intended to impress.
Are you doing what God has asked you to do? Has He answered your prayer in a specific way? Praise and thank Him for it!

Tuesday • Genesis 24:34-51

Q
A

DIGGING DEEPER • When was the last time you set aside your own physical needs to give priority to the Lord's work? That's what this faithful servant did in refusing to eat until he had explained his mission. In explaining his master's greatness, he made sure the Lord got the credit for directing his path and words. From Genesis to Revelation, the Euphrates River represents the dividing line between idol worship and the Land of Promise from which God will cast out idolatry. Abraham's brother Nahor and his family acknowledged Abraham's God, but clung to their idols as well.
Is God your only God, or is He added to other things that you worship? Skip a meal today and spend that time in prayer. Ask God to lead you or reveal to you part of His plan for your life.

Wednesday • Genesis 24:52-67

Q&A

DIGGING DEEPER • Have you ever been torn between doing something right now and waiting a while to do it? That is a little of what Rebekah faced. Rebekah had to believe and trust the messenger for all of the rest of her future. She didn't know if she'd ever see her family again. She decided to go with the servant. In order for her to enter into the covenant blessings of Abraham, she had to forsake all that she had known in the past and cross over to the Land of Promise. The journey would be long and treacherous, but she had to trust the one who sent for her and the one who was sent to bring her back. He knew the way and had provisions for the long way.
Would you be able to pack up and move on a day's notice if the Lord asked you to? For what are you trusting and believing God?

Thursday • Genesis 25:19-34

Q&A

DIGGING DEEPER • Abraham, in preparation for his death, gave gifts of his wealth to each of his sons by Hagar and Keturah and sent them far away. The Arabic people claim to be Abraham's descendants by these sons. Then Abraham gave everything else he had to Isaac. It is interesting to note the Jewish people also claim to be Abraham's descendants, but through Isaac and Jacob. Beginning here, the Scriptures will focus on Isaac and his descendants. Isaac became a digger of wells and a builder of altars like his father. We will see that he has some spiritual lapses when he regards his physical needs and safety above the spiritual values of trust and truth.
Pray for the troubles in the Middle East. This passage gives us a better understanding of how it all started and how long it's been going on.

Friday • Genesis 27:1-17

DIGGING DEEPER • Have you ever wanted something so badly that you went behind people's backs to make it happen? That's what Rebekah did. Isaac was deceived, and unaware that Esau had sold his birthright to Jacob. He wanted to grant the birthright to his favorite or eldest son, Esau, before his death. However, Rebekah was just as determined that her favorite son, Jacob, would receive the blessing, and created a deceitful plan to get it. By taking God's work into her own hands, Rebekah missed the blessing of seeing God fulfill His purpose and promise in giving Jacob the birthright and blessing in His perfect way.
Confess as sin any attempt to get your own way. Trust God with a problem you're facing right now. Let Him work it out.

Saturday • Genesis 27:18-33

DIGGING DEEPER • Did you ever have to make a decision based only on your sense of smell and touch? Isaac's sight had failed and his sense of hearing was playing tricks on him. Rebekah anticipated this. His sense of taste failed to distinguish goat from venison, and his sense of smell and touch convinced him that the right son was there. Isaac gave Jacob the blessing, advantages, privileges, and responsibilities of the firstborn. After he learned the truth, Isaac made it clear to Esau that the blessing would not be revoked. Before their birth, God had ordained that Isaac and Jacob would be the heirs of the covenant to Abraham. However, Rebekah and Jacob would pay dearly for intervening in God's plan.
If you have received Christ, thank God that you are an heir of God's kingdom. Think about your blessings, privileges, and responsibilities

qt WEEK 13

What kind of stories do you like to read? Do you prefer deceit, plans to murder, people running away from home, and exciting chases? Or would you rather read about romance, building a family, God keeping His promises, and people returning to Him? You'll read about all of these this week!

Prayer focus for this week

Q: The Question — *What is the writer saying?*
A: The Answer — *How Can I apply this to my life?*

Sunday • Genesis 27:34-45

DIGGING DEEPER • When was the last time you were really mad at your brother or sister? Were you mad enough to plan how you would kill them? Probably not! Esau was. He concluded that the only way he could regain what he considered rightfully his was through the death of his brother, Jacob. Not only was Esau deprived of the firstborn's double portion, but he was made a servant to Jacob. Compare the blessings Isaac gave to his sons. They were both to prosper, which we will see they did personally and nationally. The nation of Israel descended from Jacob, and the Edomites were Esau's descendants. When we devise plans of our own instead of trusting God, something usually goes wrong.
Read Jeremiah 10:23 and Proverbs 3:5-6 to learn how to avoid the pitfalls of making your own plans. Learn to trust God when you're in trouble.

Monday • Genesis 28:10-22

DIGGING DEEPER • When you prepare to take a long trip and you know you'll be gone a long time, what do you take with you? Almost everything! Not Jacob. There is no mention of servants, donkeys, or even provisions for his six hundred mile journey that would take him several weeks. In fact Genesis 32:10 says he only took his staff (stick). In an amazing way the Lord confirmed to Jacob the covenant previously given to Abraham and Isaac. The Lord's blessing on Jacob does not indicate that He overlooked or approved of Jacob's sinful methods. God possesses perfect foreknowledge and was able to weave Jacob's errors into the pattern of His eternal purposes.
Are you ready to go wherever the Lord leads you? Think about the many promises the Lord has given you in His Word.

Tuesday • Genesis 29:1-20

DIGGING DEEPER • Do you think this is the same well where Rebekah was found for Isaac? It is probably the very same one. Jacob's conversation in verse 7 indicates that he was trying to get the others to leave so he could be alone with Rachel. He didn't want or need everyone to hear or know his business. It is interesting to note that Isaac married Rebekah as soon as he saw her, but Jacob had to wait and work for seven years for Rachel. As a side note, there are some comparisons that can be made about Sarah, Rebekah, and Rachel. They were all closely related by blood and marriage, but never met each other; all were younger than their husbands, but died before them. God even had to miraculously open each of their wombs.
Are you careful about to whom you tell your business? How well do you know your family tree? Ask about your grandparents and their parents.

Wednesday • Genesis 31:3-18

Q&A

DIGGING DEEPER • Have you ever been somewhere you didn't feel welcome? That's how Jacob and his family were beginning to feel. The Lord told Jacob to return to the land of his father, and renewed the promise He had given to him twenty years earlier. Jacob and his wives were ready to listen and obey the Lord. They no longer felt welcomed by Laban and his sons; in fact, they felt threatened. Notice how God reminds Jacob that He was responsible for his wealth, and identifies Himself as the same God Jacob had encountered years before at Bethel. Jacob assembled his family, servants, and possessions and headed back home six hundred miles away.

Make sure visitors to your club, church, or school feel welcome. Praise God for His promises, knowing He will keep every one. Read verses 19-55.

Thursday • Genesis 32:1-12

Q&A

DIGGING DEEPER • Do you think you have family problems? Jacob had family problems coming and going! Laban chased Jacob and his family but was warned by God to do them no harm. Laban was more concerned about getting his idols back. When Jacob learned that Esau was coming with four hundred men, he was frightened. He devised a plan he hoped would save half his family. Next, Jacob prayed back to the Lord the very words that the Lord had said to him a few weeks earlier. In a good pattern of prayer for us to follow, he acknowledged God's greatness, followed by a confession of what he was in God's presence. Then, basically, he said, "Lord, I obeyed your command, so please come through with your promise."

Ask God to help you with any family problem by praying a prayer following Jacob's pattern.

Friday • Genesis 32:13-30

DIGGING DEEPER • When was the last time you made plans, prayed about it, and decided to change your plans? That's kind of what Jacob did here. Jacob was doing everything within his own power to protect himself and his family. When he was all alone that night, he wrestled with a man who may have been the Son of God in human form before He was born. The Lord had great plans for Jacob and his descendants, but Jacob needed to learn to rely totally on the Lord and not on his own strength. After wrestling with the Lord all night long, Jacob still did not submit, so the Lord crippled him with just a touch, then blessed him and changed his name to Israel.
Rely on the Lord and not your own plans. Read John 15:5 and Philippians 4:13 to see two principles we need to understand about making plans.

Saturday • Genesis 35:1-15

DIGGING DEEPER • Is there a particular place you like to visit that holds special memories of times with loved ones or with the Lord? That was Bethel to Jacob. It's the place where his grandfather, Abraham, returned after his lapse of faith in Egypt. It is also the place where Jacob saw the ladder to heaven and received the same covenant given to Abraham and Isaac. Before Jacob returned to Bethel he cleaned his camp of any idols. It was important for his household to rid themselves of their old way of life and to give their total commitment to the God of Abraham, Isaac, and Jacob.
Get rid of anything in your life that hinders your fellowship with the Lord. Is there any sin you need to confess and put behind you? Read verses 16-29.

qt WEEK 14

How can you tell whether a dream is from God or from the pizza and ice cream you ate last night? This week we'll examine four dreams and their interpretations from God. How do you think most prisoners use their time? Wait and see how one prisoner kept himself clean and usable for the Lord's work.

Prayer focus for this week

Q: The Question *What is the writer saying?*
A: The Answer *How can I apply this to my life?*

Sunday • Genesis 37:1-17

DIGGING DEEPER • Have you ever wondered what a specific dream may have meant? In Joseph's case, they were prophetic dreams. One day he would rule over his father and brothers and they would bow before him. When his brothers understood this they hated him even more. We'll see later that it actually happened. In verses 13-17 the father sent his favorite son on a mission to seek his brothers. Notice that he went willingly. There is a parallel here that can be compared with God sending His Son to seek and to save. The story of Joseph is not an allegory. Each detail given in Scripture actually happened to real people in real places at specific times.

Obey the Lord, even when you feel threatened by others who want to harm you. Tell the truth in all situations!

Monday • Genesis 37:18-36

Q
A

DIGGING DEEPER • Did you know that the Bible equates hatred with murder? Look up 1John 3:15. Notice the brothers' sequence of actions toward Joseph: they hated him (v. 4), hated him more (v. 5) and even more (v. 8), they conspired to kill him (v. 18), mocked him (v. 19), stripped him (v. 23), condemned him to die of thirst (v. 24), sat down to watch (v. 25), and rejected him for silver (v. 28). Within the Ishmaelite caravan was a group of Midianite merchantmen. (Interestingly, they were all descendants of Abraham—cousins even!) They evidently handled the transaction between the Ishmaelites and the Egyptians because they had knowledge of the language and had the trade contacts.
Confess any hatred in your heart as sin. How is your relationship with your cousins? Reach out and share Jesus with them.

Tuesday • Genesis 39:1-16

Q
A

DIGGING DEEPER • By comparing Genesis 37:2, 41:1, and 46 we find out that about ten years are represented in verses 1-7. That's a long time for Joseph to be a slave working to please his God and his owner. Look at Joseph's character: he was a commendable servant, given control of all things in the household, others were blessed through him, and although he resisted repeated temptations, he was falsely accused of having done something wrong. After all the seemingly bad things that had happened in Joseph's life, he still trusted God, worked hard, and did his best for those he served.
Could the above character qualities describe you? Trust God, work hard, and be a servant to others.

Wednesday • Genesis 39:17-40:8

DIGGING DEEPER • Have you ever been punished for something when it was really someone else's fault? That is what happened here with Joseph. He was bound and condemned because of a lie told by Potiphar's wife. There is no record that any of the other servants tried to defend him. Before the Scriptures were completed, God communicated prophetic messages in various ways. One way was through dreams. God gave two men in the Old Testament the ability to interpret the dreams of others—Joseph and Daniel. Therefore, when two important prisoners under his care reported mysterious dreams on the same night, Joseph was anxious to determine whether they were from God.

Are you ready to be punished for doing the right thing? Today God speaks to us mainly through His Word. How much time do you spend listening?

Thursday • Genesis 40:9-23

DIGGING DEEPER • What could have happened to make the king (Pharaoh) mad at the trusted servants who were closest to him? The chief butler, or cupbearer, and the chief baker would have worked long and hard to earn such honored positions in the palace. One thought is that a plot was discovered to assassinate him with poison, and that these two servants were the chief suspects. Then, three days before Pharaoh's birthday it was discovered who the guilty person really was. God got the glory when He gave the men their dreams and gave the interpretations to Joseph. Unfortunately, the butler forgot about Joseph, and he remained in prison continuing to do his job to the best of his ability.

Is anyone mad at you, or are you mad at anyone? Set it right. Do the job God has given you to the best of your ability, trusting Him for the outcome.

Friday • Genesis 41:1-16

DIGGING DEEPER • This is the fourth time in Genesis that God has brought about His purposes in the life of one of His servants through the dreams of other people. In the first two occasions (20:3 and 31:24), the dreamers realized the message was from God and understood the message. In 40:5 and 41:1, the dreams were a complete mystery to the dreamers, so God brought about the circumstances so that His servant Joseph would be the interpreter. Joseph used the opportunities to explain that he couldn't interpret the dreams himself, but that God might give him the explanations. As we'll see in God's program, the way up is down, meaning we need to serve others and let God bring us up (Proverbs 16:18).
Are you in any circumstances in which God could use you to help someone else understand Him better or grow closer to Him?

Saturday • Genesis 41:17-36

DIGGING DEEPER • Joseph is finally out of the dungeon! However, he finds himself in the presence of the most powerful person of his time. Immediately after hearing Pharaoh's dream, Joseph interprets it for him. In a few words, he tells Pharaoh about what is going to come upon him and his nation in the next fourteen years. Notice that Joseph emphasizes four times that the message is from God. Without a pause, Joseph proceeds to counsel the king in the presence of his advisors. Such confidence can only come from an assurance that he is speaking words given to him by God. In his years as a slave, Joseph kept himself clean and useable for his God.
Keep yourself clean and usable for God regardless of the circumstances, testing, or pressure you face. Be ready to tell others what God says.

qt WEEK 15

Do you have brothers? You can have a lot of fun or get into trouble with them. Sometimes they can be harsh and, other times, overprotective. They can be your best friends and sometimes your worst enemies. This week we'll see several dynamics that Joseph and his brothers have to work through.

Prayer focus for this week

Q: The Question — *What is the writer saying?*
A: The Answer — *How Can I apply this to my life?*

Sunday • Genesis 41:37-57

Q
A

DIGGING DEEPER • Joseph is the most complete type in Scripture of the coming Lord Jesus Christ. More than fifty parallels can be found between the two. In this passage alone, we see that Joseph rose from condemnation and was highly exalted. He found favor with God and man. He was declared to be above all others in wisdom, and revealed what was going to come. He was given supreme authority in the land and given fine linen and gold to wear. Every knee bowed before him. Students of the life of Christ will recognize that every statement made above about Joseph has a scriptural parallel concerning Jesus Christ. As a man, Joseph was a sinner, but God chose not to disclose any of his faults in His Word.
Do others see Jesus in you? What are you doing to become more like Christ? We have the advantage of having the Holy Spirit living in us to help.

Monday • Genesis 42:1-20

Q
A

DIGGING DEEPER • Joseph's brothers had last seen him as a seventeen-year-old pest. If they thought about or looked for him at all, it would have been among the slaves of the land. They may have thought he had died. Now Joseph was around forty, and his speech, dress, and clean shaven face were that of an Egyptian. Joseph had two purposes in his harsh treatment of his brothers: first, to see his brother Benjamin, and secondly, to test the repentance of his brothers. In his first dream, eleven brothers bowed down to him. If it were truly from God it would be fulfilled. God had a purpose for these men, but they had to repent of their sin and bow down before it could happen.
How do you treat your siblings? Show them God's love today. Is there any sin you need to confess? Do it and look for God's purpose in your life.

Tuesday • Genesis 42:21-38

Q
A

DIGGING DEEPER • Did you ever do something wrong, cover it up, and think you got away with it...until later when it was revealed and you got into bigger trouble? The nine brothers who had conspired against Joseph confessed the sin they had committed more than twenty years ago. Reuben reminded them that there would be consequences for their actions. They were certain that God had not forgotten their sin and was orchestrating this chain of events, and they were rightfully worried. Joseph heard what they had to say, but wanted to know if they were genuinely sorry. By returning their money, Joseph showed that his favor could not be bought. It had to be received as a gift.
Confess any sin that you may think you got away with. God knows all about it! Are you prepared to suffer the consequences?

Wednesday • Genesis 43:1-15

DIGGING DEEPER • Have you ever changed your mind about something? You thought one way about something, then you got more information and you had to change your mind? Joseph's brothers have had to deal with their father's grief and overprotection of their brother Benjamin for over twenty years. In that time, they went from brothers who hated Joseph and wanted him out of their lives, even selling him into slavery, to brothers who pledged their lives and the lives of their own children to protect Joseph's brother, Benjamin. The Bible doesn't tell us how much time passed between the first trip to Egypt to buy food and the second trip, but it is obvious it was a while, because they were getting desperate for food.
About what do you need to change your mind? God loves you and has a plan for your life; ask Him to help you.

Thursday • Genesis 43:16-34

DIGGING DEEPER • Isn't it hard to be patient with people when you want to confront them about something you think they did wrong, but you have to wait and let things work out? Joseph's eleven brothers were there before him, bowing down to him just like in his dream (chapter 37), but he wasn't satisfied yet. He needed to know whether they were truly sorry for selling him into slavery, and what their relationship to Benjamin was like. How had they treated Benjamin all these years? Think about it, what would you have thought if you were Joseph? He probably assumed that his brothers had treated Benjamin the same way they had treated him, or maybe even worse.
Do something special for your siblings to let them know you love and appreciate them. Thank God for the family He's put you in.

Friday • Genesis 44:1-17

Q
A

DIGGING DEEPER • The brothers must have felt a lot better on the way home this time than after the first trip. The first time, they had been falsely accused, imprisoned, and forced to leave Simeon as a hostage. This time, their gift was received, they were cleared from all charges, and Simeon was restored to them. They were treated to a special dinner, given plenty of provisions, and were taking Benjamin safely back to their father. However, due to circumstantial evidence, it looked like Benjamin had stolen the Egyptian's silver cup and was going to have to stay in Egypt as his slave. What do you think was going through the minds of the ten brothers? **How do you respond when you're falsely accused? Have you ever falsely accused someone, only to find out later he didn't do it? Determine to live your life by always telling the truth.**

Saturday • Genesis 44:18-34

Q
A

DIGGING DEEPER • What would you choose if given the choice between going home free or becoming a slave in a foreign country? Joseph's brothers were given this very choice. They could freely go home if they were willing to turn Benjamin over to the same fate to which they had turned Joseph over so many years earlier. Judah stepped up and preferred slavery in Egypt over the freedom that would have heaped guilt upon guilt for him. He knew he couldn't face his father without Benjamin with him. In honoring his pledge to his father, he showed his repentance and offered himself in place of Benjamin.
Do you have a hard choice to make? Ask God for the wisdom to make the right choice.

qt WEEK 16

There are many important events that happen in a family. One of the biggest is moving, which involves finding the best place to live. This week, a special place is provided for a family. You'll also find out what happens to make family members speechless, and some special blessings that are given on a deathbed.

Prayer focus for this week

Q: The Question — *What is the writer saying?*
A: The Answer — *How Can I apply this to my life?*

Sunday • Genesis 45:1-15

DIGGING DEEPER • Have you ever been shocked by something that you were utterly speechless? When Joseph was convinced that his brothers were truly sorry for what they had done to him, he could no longer control his pent-up emotions, and revealed to them who he was. They were speechless! How could this possibly be their brother, Joseph? They may have felt that now they would surely be punished for their sin against him. They deserved to suffer as slaves, but Joseph had already paid that penalty for them (Psalm 105:17-18). Now they just needed to embrace Joseph and learn to comprehend his love, forgiveness, and the protection he offered.

Have you ever felt guilty even after you confessed your sin? Read Psalm 32 to find out how forgiveness and restoration can be yours.

Monday • Genesis 45:16-28

Q & A

DIGGING DEEPER • We can see the truth of Proverbs 21:1 in these verses. Pharaoh supplied protection and material for God's people so they could perform God's purposes on the Earth. Joseph sent his brothers home to tell their father that he was alive and that Jacob (Israel) needed to move to Egypt to be cared for and protected from the severe famine. It's humorous to note that Joseph told them not to argue on the way home. He probably anticipated that they would be blaming one another for what they had done to Joseph. Can you imagine their conversations as to who would tell and what exactly to tell their father about Joseph?
What has God supplied for you through others? Thank them for it! Tell others this story of deliverance today and encourage them to trust God.

Tuesday • Genesis 46:1-6; 28-30

Q & A

DIGGING DEEPER • Is there a special place your family likes to go? Beer-sheba was a special place and held significance for Abraham, Isaac, and Jacob. It was from there that Jacob left to spend twenty years with his Uncle Laban. Before leaving the Promised Land, Jacob stopped at Beer-sheba to worship the one true God. God honored Jacob's act of faith by speaking to him for the seventh time in his life. God assured him of His presence and of the fulfillment of His covenant to Abraham and Isaac. Jacob said he was ready to die after he saw Joseph; but in reality he lived another seventeen years.
God promises to be with His people (Matthew 28:20; John 14:3). Trust God to provide for you and protect you in whatever circumstances you face.

Wednesday • Genesis 47:1-12; 27-31

Q&A

DIGGING DEEPER • Is it important where you live? Most parents try to choose the best possible place for their children to grow up. The land of Goshen was a fertile area in the eastern part of the Nile delta. It was separated from the main part of Egypt by a Nile estuary that watered it. In giving this land to his family, Joseph (through God's leading) provided a way to keep his family separated from the Egyptians in order to prevent them from being tempted into the Egyptian culture. Jacob's final desire was to be buried in the Promised Land. God may have provided for him in Egypt, but his heart was still in the Promised Land.
From what part of our culture do you need to be separated? Where is your heart? Ask God to guide you as to where it would be best to spend your time. What are some things you should avoid?

Thursday • Genesis 48:1-16

Q&A

DIGGING DEEPER • What people have to say on their death beds is very important to the family around them. When Joseph heard that Jacob was very sick and may be on his death bed, he brought his two sons to him to be blessed. In that culture, this was the time and place at which the Patriarch gave special blessings, rights, and responsibilities to his children. Jacob granted a double portion of the birthright to Joseph by making his two sons equal to Jacob's other eleven sons. In doing so Joseph would father two tribes of Israel and his brothers would get one tribe each.
What blessings, rights, and responsibilities do you have as a child of God? Read Galatians 5:16 to see how we are to walk as God's children.

Friday • Genesis 49:8-10; 22-28

DIGGING DEEPER • Just before he died, Jacob gathered his twelve sons around his bed and spoke prophetic words to them concerning the twelve tribes which would descend from them as his sons. The prominence given to Judah and to Joseph is easily detected. The Messianic line through which Jesus Christ would come was promised to Judah. Joseph received the birthright usually given to the first born. Later when the Promised Land was divided up to the different tribes under Joshua, the descendants of Judah and Joseph far outnumbered those of the other tribes. They were also given more land, which was more strategically located. **What blessing or inheritance are you expecting? Do you have the blessing and inheritance of being a child of God? If not, you can ask for it today.**

Saturday • Genesis 50:7-26

DIGGING DEEPER • Jacob's body was embalmed in Egypt and taken with great ceremony to the Promised Land. He was buried in the cave at the edge of a field or plain called Machpelah, which Abraham bought (Genesis 23:9-11). He was buried with Abraham and Sarah, Isaac and Rebekah, and with his wife Leah. Did you notice the brothers were still worried that Joseph may punish them even seventeen years after he had completely and unconditionally forgiven them? They were still trying to work their way into his favor by offering to be his servants. They could have had rest and comfort and been free from fear if they had just believed Joseph's words. **Do you know where you will go when you die? Your body will probably go in the ground, but where will your spirit go? Are you accepting God's gift of forgiveness and salvation, or trying to work your way to Heaven?**

qt WEEK 17

Do you like surprises? You are going to enjoy reading Matthew this week. The surprises just keep coming. You will read about the birth of the Messiah, the first birthday party, the message of a new kingdom, the traps of Satan, and a strange choice of messengers. How many surprises can you take?

Prayer focus for this week

Q: The Question *What is the writer saying?*
A: The Answer *How Can I apply this to my life?*

Sunday • Matthew 1:1-17

DIGGING DEEPER • Have you ever researched your family tree? Some people find they have relatives in their past who were not hallmark citizens. Today, Matthew gave his readers Jesus' family tree. Not only are most of the names hard to pronounce, (how would you feel if your parents named you "Zorobabel"!) but there are a few surprises: Thamar (Tamar) (the deceiver), Rachab (Rahab) (the harlot), Ruth (the foreigner), and Bathsheba (the adulterer). It is a wonderful thing to experience the awesome grace of God in your life. It is even greater to realize that God's grace reaches over all ethnic and cultural walls to change people's lives forever.
What person has the Holy Spirit brought to your mind? How is that person different from you? Ask God to show you how to share His Gospel with that person this week.

Monday • Matthew 1:18-25

DIGGING DEEPER • What would your advice be if an unmarried friend told you she was pregnant? Once again, we see the grace of God, for without an intervention from God, Mary and Joseph may have had different reactions. Matthew shows us the character of Mary and Joseph. Mary was willing to submit to the perfect will of God, even though she did not quite understand what was happening. Joseph was willing to submit to the will of God by accepting Mary, who would have a child that was not his. The times when we do not understand what God is doing in our lives are the hardest times to trust in God's Word. Do you have the kind of character that God would display to bring glory and honor to His name? **What kind of character do you have? Ask God what He thinks of your character, and then take the time to listen to His still, small voice.**

Tuesday • Matthew 2:1-12

DIGGING DEEPER • How would you feel if an important government official visited your home? In our passage today, wise men came to visit Jesus. These wise men traveled far to see the baby who is known as the King of the Jews. They had followed a star which had been shining in the east and led them to Jerusalem. They stopped to ask King Herod; surely he would know where this new King was living. The king had to ask his advisors. It seemed no one really cared about this new King. When they left the king, they saw the star which led them right to Jesus. They brought three gifts: gold (a king's gift), frankincense (a very expensive perfume), and myrrh (a perfume used in burials).
How brightly are you shining? Examine your life. Is your life shining brightly enough to lead others to Jesus?

Wednesday • Matthew 2:13-23

Q&A

DIGGING DEEPER • Do you find it hard to trust someone when you are not sure of the outcome? God instructed Joseph to pack up his family and move to Egypt because Herod was out to kill Jesus. Then, a few years later, God instructed Joseph to move his family back to Israel. During the second move, Joseph became concerned when he learned that Archelaus (Herod's son) was in charge. It would be much easier to trust God if He would give us the whole plan with dates of events up front. We must remember that God is interested in our personal growth, so He gives us opportunities to grow. How much faith does it take to do something when you already know the outcome? When God impresses upon our hearts to make a move, He is allowing us to grow in our trust of His protection and provision. **What is God asking you to do? Will you trust God with your whole life?**

Thursday • Matthew 3:1-17

Q&A

DIGGING DEEPER • Have you ever had news you were just busting to tell? John knew about the coming Messiah (Jesus) and the work He would do through the Holy Spirit. One day Jesus will collect His family, as a farmer collects grains of wheat during harvest time. Those who reject Jesus will suffer destruction, just as wheat hulls fly into a fire. John knew the Messiah was coming and wanted everyone to prepare. Those who refused to prepare would end up like the hulls of wheat. Judgment was coming, and there was only one way out. We have the same message; Jesus is coming to collect His family, and those who refuse to become part of His family face destruction. Are you part of Jesus' family?
Ask God to put someone in your path this week who needs to hear your testimony of Jesus.

Friday • Matthew 4:1-11

Q
A

DIGGING DEEPER • Satan works through many avenues of temptation, and many times this temptation catches us off guard. Maybe it's in the form of a lie to our parents, taking something small that no one will ever miss, or some porn that pops up while we're working on the computer. It is important for us to keep our guard up at all times, just as Jesus did. Even though he was tired and hungry, He did not step into Satan's trap; He used the power of the Holy Spirit to resist. Satan works on our mind to convince us that this sin is a small one and no one will ever know. Then, as soon as we step into the trap, Satan begins to make us feel guilty. His trap worked, and it seems there is no way out. Keep your guard up!
Ask God to help you keep your spiritual eyes open so you can see Satan's traps and resist them through the power of the Holy Spirit.

Saturday • Matthew 4:12-25

Q
A

DIGGING DEEPER • Have you ever felt your way around in the dark, trying to find a light? This is a very helpless feeling. People who are without Christ are feeling their way through the darkness trying to find some kind of light. In today's section, Jesus began preaching about the kingdom and recruiting men to take His light to people living in darkness. The feeling a person experiences when he finds Jesus is like the feeling of relief you get when you finally find some light in that pitch darkness. Jesus is still sending out light carriers (disciples) into the darkness, bringing relief and hope to those who see no hope. Remember the feeling of release from anxiety or tension, or the lightness and cheerfulness that came over you when you found Jesus? Jesus has chosen you to share His light in your world.
What ways to share Jesus' light can you think of today?

qt WEEK 18

Have you ever watched a caterpillar surround himself with a cocoon and then some time later emerge as a beautiful butterfly? What a great picture of God surrounding us with His grace and love, then helping us emerge as new creatures. Do not read your quiet time this week unless you are ready to change!

Prayer focus for this week

Q: The Question — *What is the writer saying?*
A: The Answer — *How Can I apply this to my life?*

Sunday • Matthew 5:1-16

Q
A

DIGGING DEEPER • Heart transplants have lengthened or saved many lives; however, heart transplants do not change the character of a person. In today's passage, Jesus is dealing with a heart change through a mind change. Before a person can change the way he lives, he must change the way he thinks. Jesus is talking about making a radical change in your thinking process. As you read the verses, make a mental note of the change in thinking; blessed are the meek, blessed are the pure in heart, and blessed are the merciful. Jesus is saying that before you can make a change in your behavior (character), you must change your thinking. God has a tough demand on righteousness. Are you ready to follow Jesus Christ?
As you think through the day, does your thinking match God's way of thinking? Ask God to help you change your thinking process (character).

Monday • Matthew 5:17-32

Q
A

DIGGING DEEPER • Sometimes we say things to people who interpret what we said into an entirely different meaning. Jesus is continuing with the thinking theme, but He is facing the same problem. He told the Jews that He had not come to do away with the law by any means. He had come to fulfill the law; to take it one step further. The scribes and Pharisees were just concerned with the outward appearance, but Jesus told them that the outward appearance can fool you. That is why God is concerned with the thinking process of a man. Then He used several examples; one was killing. Jesus said it is not enough to say that killing someone is wrong, but even to think about killing someone is wrong. That is a radical change.
Is your righteousness only skin deep? Examine your life today. Do you live righteously because you think that way, or to fool others?

Tuesday • Matthew 5:33-48

Q
A

DIGGING DEEPER • Have you ever made someone swear he is telling the truth? Have you ever wanted to pay someone back for something he did to you? Have you ever tried to help someone who hated you? These are very piercing questions. In today's passage Jesus tells us to be known as people who tell the truth. Then there are those times when paying someone back for the pain or embarrassment he caused would be so satisfying. However, Jesus tells us to help those who have needs, even if they are hateful people. Finally, Jesus says it is no special thing to love those who love you; however, it is special when you love someone who hates or uses you.
Loving people is a matter of determination. What person who dislikes you is the Holy Spirit bringing to your mind? Show him love today.

Wednesday • Matthew 6:1-18

DIGGING DEEPER • In today's culture, people worship all kinds of things: cars, money, houses, fame, glory, and success. Today, Jesus gives the secret to real worship. Worship is not about outward things performed to get attention, such as giving money, praying in public, or fasting (going without food for a certain period) and telling people so they will think, Isn't he spiritual. Real worship happens when a person performs acts out of love for the Lord that no one else may know about. The outward appearance is important because it is a picture of what is happening on the inside. True worship of God starts inside a person with his attitude toward God. **Are you just acting out the Christian life? God is looking at the attitude of your heart. What does He see? Take time to search your heart. Whom are you trying to please?**

Thursday • Matthew 6:19-34

DIGGING DEEPER • In the movie Shenandoah, Jimmy Stewart is sitting with his family around the supper table and prays something like this: "Now, God, we did all the planting, and all the caring, and all the harvesting of this food without any help from you, but we thank you for it anyway." He missed the principle in today's passage. What can God tell people He owns? One of Satan's traps is to convince people that they own the things they have. Today Jesus is attempting to change the way we think about our possessions. Everything we have belongs to God. He is allowing us to take care of a piece of His property for a little while. When things become yours, you become a clinger instead of resting in God's ability to provide. **What possessions are you unwilling to give back to God? Take your most prized possession and give it back to God today.**

Friday • Matthew 7:1-12

Q
A

DIGGING DEEPER • Can you remember something that you did that was foolish? Yeah, we all can. Today Jesus talks about foolish things people do. First, He talks about those people who do foolish things and then try to correct someone else who is doing something foolish. It is kind of like a father chewing tobacco while standing in front of his sons cautioning them not to take up smoking. Second, He talks about throwing nice jewelry into a pigpen expecting the pigs to wear it. Third, He talks about a man giving a rock or a serpent to his children when they ask for food. All of these acts are foolish, and while we do foolish things, God never does. When we go to God in prayer, He never makes us feel like fools.
God says for us to treat people the way we want them to treat us. Whom has God brought into your life whom you need to treat differently?

Saturday • Matthew 7:13-29

Q
A

DIGGING DEEPER • In Tornado Alley, the towns are filled with tornado sirens. When a siren goes off, it is a warning that danger is fast approaching. Those who choose to ignore the warning will find themselves in a mess of trouble. Those who heed the warnings find safety. In our passage today, Jesus gives four warnings to those seeking the kingdom: First, there is a narrow way into the kingdom. Second, watch out for teachers who teach false doctrine. Third, check your life for bad fruit. Fourth, make sure you are building on a solid foundation. Warning signals are very important – they help us avoid danger, but only if we pay attention to them. Are you on the only path that leads to heaven?
God gives us warning signs to help us get on the right path and stay on the right path. What warning signs in your life are you ignoring today?

qt WEEK 19

One of the greatest things about the Christian life is the grace of God. As you read this week, you will see time and time again where God's grace is given to those who need it. Without the grace of God, no person would ever step foot into heaven. Enjoy God's grace this week.

Prayer focus for this week

Q: The Question — *What is the writer saying?*
A: The Answer — *How Can I apply this to my life?*

Sunday • Matthew 8:1-17

DIGGING DEEPER • Just think, what would happen if there were a place where cancer patients could go and have someone touch them and heal them completely? That place would be crowded night and day, with people lined up for their cures. In today's passage, Jesus cured hopeless people from their diseases. As you read, pay close attention to the progression of the miracles. First, there was the leper, a Jew – a picture of Jesus coming to the Jews, who rejected His offer of the kingdom. Next, there was the centurion, a Gentile – a picture of Jesus opening the door of salvation to the Gentiles. Finally, there was Peter's mother-in-law, a Jew – a picture of Jesus going back to the Jews with His offer of the kingdom.
We are in the second picture and the door is wide open to come to Jesus for salvation. Have you accepted Jesus as your personal Savior?

Monday • Matthew 8:18-34

DIGGING DEEPER • Have you ever felt you should be able to clean your room when you want, not when your mother wants you to? In today's passage Jesus talked with people who wanted to follow Him the way they wanted to, not Jesus' way. One man refused to follow Jesus because Jesus did not have a place to live. Who wants to live outside? Another man refuses to follow Jesus because Jesus would not wait until it was convenient for him to leave his family. The disciples were not sure what to do, either; they had never seen anyone control nature like this man. Finally, a whole town asked Jesus to leave because He had destroyed their means of making a living when He killed all the pigs. Following Jesus is not always convenient.
Do not wait until it's convenient to follow. Give Jesus all of your life today.

Tuesday • Matthew 9:1-13

DIGGING DEEPER • When you are sick and go to the doctor, does he give you medicine for your runny nose, sore throat, or aching head? No, those are just the symptoms of what you have. The doctor gives you medicine to cure your infection; with the infection cured, the symptoms disappear. That is what Jesus did in today's passage. The paralyzed man's problem was not that he was paralyzed; instead, it was his sin. Jesus cured the sin problem by telling the man his sins were forgiven. Once freed from the sin, he could walk. The symptoms disappeared when the virus was destroyed.
Living in sin is like trying to walk in quicksand; the harder you try, the farther down you sink. Allow Jesus to cleanse you life from sin today. Start walking with Him again.

Wednesday • Matthew 9:14-26

Q&A

DIGGING DEEPER • There are many things that, when mixed together, produce better products. Chocolate and peanut butter make a great peanut butter cup; coke and vanilla make a great soft drink. However, trying to mix oil and water is impossible. They just do not go together. In today's passage, Jesus taught the disciples that you cannot mix law and grace. They just do not fit together. Jesus was offering the kingdom, something new, which could not fit into the old Jewish system. Today, Jesus is offering people grace, something that cannot fit into the old system of law. Grace is far better than law because humanity cannot keep the law, but through God's grace, humanity can spend eternity with God in heaven. **Through grace, God gives new life to those who accept His Son. Are you experiencing God's grace in your life today?**

Thursday • Matthew 9:27-38

Q&A

DIGGING DEEPER • God, I cannot do that; I am too dumb, too shy, too poor, and too scared. What excuse are you giving God for not serving Him with your life? In today's passage, Jesus healed two blind men, cast a devil out of another person, and healed many others. Then He looked over the multitude of people and His heart broke. Jesus saw a world full of people that needed someone to care about them. With a broken heart, Jesus told the disciples to look at the crowds and see the scores of people who were crying out for help. Pray for God to send out more workers into the fields to reach the people that are crying out for help. They're everywhere – who is going to reach them? **Jesus is not looking for people to reach, He is looking for people to work. Stop giving Jesus excuses and let Him work through you to reach others.**

Friday • Matthew 10:1-15

Q&A

DIGGING DEEPER • David Brainerd was kicked out of Yale University, he had tuberculosis that took his life at the age of twenty-seven, yet he became the greatest missionary to the American Indians we have ever known. To those whom God gives much, He expects much in return. In our country, we are given much. Many Christian teenagers in our country are raised in a Christian home, go to a Christian school, and attend a Christian college; however, serving Christ with their lives may be the last thing on their minds. Jesus has sent us on a mission to tell others about the good news of salvation. Are you fulfilling your responsibility? To whom much is given, much will be required.
Take a few moments to think about how much God has given you. Now answer this question: How much am I giving back to God?

Saturday • Matthew 10:16-31

Q&A

DIGGING DEEPER • Church history gives us examples of saints down through the ages who gave everything they possessed for their belief in Christ. Many gave their lives, some were hanged, others tortured in unbelievable ways, and many burned at the stake. In today's passage, Jesus told His disciples to expect that kind of treatment. Even today, in parts of our world, people are still giving their lives for their faith in Christ. The Bible tells us this will happen again on a much greater scale during the Tribulation period. Just remember, God is in control. While we may not understand why, we must learn to trust in God's love for us.
What does your future hold? Only God knows the answer to that; however, the neat thing is that the God who knows is also the God who is in control. Put your life completely in God's hands today and trust in His love for you.

qt WEEK 20

Decisions, decisions, decisions! This is a week full of decision-making. Jesus does not allow people to stand in the middle of the road; there are decisions to be made, and each of us must make them. The Holy Spirit will ask you this week – What are you going to do with Jesus?

Prayer focus for this week

Q: The Question — *What is the writer saying?*
A: The Answer — *How Can I apply this to my life?*

Sunday • Matthew 10:32-42

DIGGING DEEPER • Thomas Cranmer was sentenced by Queen Mary I to die for his belief in Jesus Christ. On the day he was sentenced to die, he was allowed to speak to the crowd. In his speech, he talked about how Jesus changed his life and that the Pope was not more important than Jesus Christ. Many people rushed the platform, grabbing Thomas to carry him away. Thomas Cranmer broke loose from the crowd and ran to the burning post waiting for the followers of the Queen to set the fire. To Thomas Cranmer, taking a stand for Christ was more important even than life itself. Thomas Cranmer became one of three lights in England that burn for Christ even six centuries later.

Are you willing to confess Christ in front of your friends and family today? Today, when your opportunity comes, do not run. Instead, stand for Christ.

Monday • Matthew 11:1-19

Q&A

DIGGING DEEPER • Have you ever stood in the middle of a seesaw and tried to balance it? What looks easy can be very difficult, because one small tilt of weight sends one end of the seesaw right to the ground. Some times balancing our attitudes and perspective can be just as difficult. In today's passage, John was beginning to doubt Jesus, maybe because he was expecting the Messiah to overthrow the Romans. Maybe there are times when we begin to doubt Jesus because He has not answered our prayers as fast as we want. Then our attitude begins to change and, before long, all we can do is complain.
Do not lose your faith in Jesus' ability to keep His word. Things may look bad where you are now, but remember Jesus is in control and has your best interest in mind.

Tuesday • Matthew 11:20-30

Q&A

DIGGING DEEPER • All across the world, men have built lighthouses on dangerous shorelines to help captains steer their ships past rocks that could sink them. With every lighthouse there must be someone to make sure the light is shining brightly, especially during a storm. The responsibility of the lighthouse worker is great. If the lighthouse worker shuns his responsibility, then captains miss the opportunity to avoid destruction. Jesus is the light of the world, and as Christians we have been given the responsibility to make sure His light is shining through us. If we shun our responsibility of shining His light, people miss the opportunity to change directions in their lives.
We possess much light, and to whom much is given, much is required. Let's have a lighthouse check. Are you fulfilling your responsibility?

Wednesday • Matthew 12:1-13

DIGGING DEEPER • Every family has some traditions. Can you name some of yours? Religion can develop traditions also, and in today's passage the Pharisees confronted Jesus about some of their traditions that He was breaking. Jesus explained to the crowd that traditions, while they have their place, are not more important than the work of God. When we try to base salvation on things people do, then we are acting like the Pharisees. God's grace is greater than any act we do for Him. It is our nature to judge people based on how we think they should act; therefore, we must be careful not to decide someone's spiritual maturity or salvation based on their actions. We don't know their motive.
Learn to spend more time enjoying God's grace in your life than worrying about God's grace in someone else's life.

Thursday • Matthew 12:14-29

DIGGING DEEPER • Have you ever tried to help someone, only to find your actions were misinterpreted? That is what happened to Jesus. First, He healed a man with a withered hand. Second, He healed a man possessed with demons. While the crowd was wondering if this man really was the "Son of David," a Jewish name for the Messiah, the Pharisees accused Jesus of working for "Beelzebub," the devil. Then Jesus explained how silly that statement was. If you cast out your own people, then the work will fail. If Satan cast out his own demons, then he would lose everything. The Pharisees were really working hard to convince the people that Jesus was a fake.
When people falsely accuse you, do you quit and go somewhere to hide? This week, do not let the devil stop you from telling others about Jesus.

Friday • Matthew 12:30-42

DIGGING DEEPER • Have you ever traveled down a road, not really knowing where you were, when suddenly you came across a fork in the road? At that moment you had to make a decision: which way to go. Today, Jesus brings the Pharisees to a fork in the road; they must decide who Jesus is. He is either the Son of God, as He claims, or He is a fake. A decision must be made. Jesus then tells them that every man will be judged by his very own words. Jesus adds that this very generation will be judged according to their words, and the Gentiles will judge them. Then Jesus gives them their last sign. He would spend three days in the heart of the earth and then return just as Jonah did from the belly of the whale. **If you are at a fork in the road spiritually, you have a decision to make. Will you follow Jesus or will you follow Satan? Choose to follow Jesus.**

Saturday • Matthew 12:43-50

DIGGING DEEPER • If you have ever raised a pig, you know that you can clean up a pig real pretty, but when you let him go, he heads right back for the mud. Today, Jesus tells the Jews that they look good on the outside, but are still wicked on the inside. Jesus is helping the Jews understand that if you do not change a man on the inside, he will always return to his sin. While the Jews were religious on the outside, they had rejected Jesus on the inside. God sees the inside man; that is how you know who a person really is. When people see you, are they looking at the dressed-up version, or are they seeing a person who is different on the inside? **Family relations cannot make us a Christian or even a good person. Do you have a personal relationship with Jesus Christ? Does your change flow from the inside, or do you just look good on the outside?**

WEEK 21

God's power is amazing, yet He uses His power to help us fulfill our responsibilities of living a godly life. We can experience God's power every day in our life through prayer. This week Jesus teaches us how to pray.

Prayer focus for this week

Q: The Question — *What is the writer saying?*
A: The Answer — *How Can I apply this to my life?*

Sunday • Matthew 13:1-23

DIGGING DEEPER • Have you ever given someone advice, only to see them reject your advice and do what they wanted to do in the first place? This same type of thing happened to Jesus. He offered the kingdom to the Jews and they rejected His offer, thinking they would find something better later. Jesus talks about why He teaches through parables from this point on. The idea is that those who want to learn will be able to seek, find, and understand, while those who want to do their own thing can just go right on their merry little way. The sower's responsibility is to give out the seed. The receiver's responsibility is to accept the seed. Neither the sower nor the receiver can do the other person's job.

God's children are responsible to sow the Gospel. We are not responsible for people's decisions. Are you fulfilling your responsibility? Be a sower!

Monday • Matthew 13:24-43

DIGGING DEEPER • Have you ever planted a garden, only to find that weeds seem to grow every day no matter how hard you work at keeping them from growing? Sometimes in your attempt to remove the weeds, you find that you pulled a good plant up by mistake. In today's passage, Jesus planted His seed (the Gospel) in the world, and while He planted good seed, Satan planted weeds. There are those who desire to pull up the weeds, but Jesus told them that His reapers would take care of that job when the harvest time comes. The reason Jesus wants to wait is because in our cleaning process, we may pull up a good plant, and that would be a waste. The reapers will do the job right with no mistakes.
The Christian's job is to sow, not reap. Stop wasting your time trying to do someone else's job; just sow the Gospel as often as you can.

Tuesday • Matthew 13:44-58

DIGGING DEEPER • Can you imagine what it must have been like during the California Gold Rush? People spent days, weeks, months, and even years searching the land for gold. When they finally found some gold they would sell everything they owned to buy that piece of land, which would give them the rights to the gold found there. In today's passage we have something similar as we see what Jesus has done for Israel. After the Jews rejected Him, He scattered (hid) Israel throughout the earth. Then Jesus gave the most precious thing He had (His life) to purchase the earth. One day He will return to claim the treasure He has hidden there. Part of that treasure is His church, which one day He will return to claim, also.
While you cannot be part of Israel unless you are born a Jew, you can become part of the church. Make sure Jesus is coming back for you.

Wednesday • Matthew 14:1-21

Q&A

DIGGING DEEPER • One of the hardest things to overcome is the terrible feeling you have when someone mistreats you. The second hardest is when someone mistreats those you love. In today's passage, Jesus heard about the death of John the Baptist. John and Jesus were first cousins. This was someone Jesus loved very much, and now Herod has taken his life for no cause. Though Jesus was hurt inside, He could not allow the circumstances about Him to stop His work for the Father. He took the disciples out for a time of rest, and then He showed them His power by feeding over 5,000 people with two fish and five loaves of bread. He was still meeting the needs of people.

It is easy to let things that happen to us or to those we love stop us from serving God. Remember, God is bigger than the circumstances.

Thursday • Matthew 14:22-36

Q&A

DIGGING DEEPER • It is amazing to see the incredible things guys do in a Strong Man Contest. One of the most remarkable feats to watch is when they pick up those huge round stones and lift them above their heads to set them on a column. Their power is just astounding. Yesterday, the disciples saw Jesus' power to feed 5,000 people with two fish and five loaves of bread, yet they were not impressed. Today, they see Jesus walk on water and calm a storm. They even see Peter walk on water! With these acts, they are impressed to the point of falling on their faces and worshiping Jesus Christ as their Lord. We see Jesus' power to change lives each time someone accepts Him as his Savior.

Do not allow the power of God to pass by and go unnoticed. Look for ways in which Jesus is demonstrating His power today.

Friday • Matthew 15:1-20

Q&A

DIGGING DEEPER • It seems that eating dirt is part of growing up. Almost every kid has eaten a mouth full of dirt at one time or another. For clean freaks, this thought throws them into a state of panic. Most of us have been taught that we should never eat anything unless we wash our hands first. Even if you have worked with gloves on all day before you eat, you must wash your hands. It has become a ritual. In Jesus' day, they had rituals, also. Many were about religion. In our passage today, the Pharisees questioned Jesus about one of these rituals. Jesus told them that it is not what a man eats, but that which is in his heart that defiles him,. What you eat does not make you who you are!
True worship of Jesus comes from within your heart, not from the things you do. Check out your life today. What rituals are you keeping for show?

Saturday • Matthew 15:21-39

Q&A

DIGGING DEEPER • Have you discovered yet that when asking your father or mother for something, it is all in the approach? If you demand something, they tend to ignore you; if you ask nicely, they may give you what you want. However, asking in a loving, caring way usually gets the best results. The woman in our story today was a Gentile, and she first addressed Jesus as if she were Jewish (thou Son of David). Then she just asked for help, and Jesus told her He was sent to help the Jews. Finally, she cried out for mercy, and Jesus responded to her cry. Then Jesus showed His power to meet needs by feeding four thousand people with a few fish and seven loaves of bread. Again, Jesus showed His power to overcome circumstances.
God answers prayer; however, the way we approach God in prayer is very important. Do you demand of God, or ask humbly?

qt WEEK 22

Why is it important to know what you believe and why you believe? That is a good question, and this week God is going to show why doctrine is important to our Christian life. In addition, this week Jesus deals with the question of divorce. Do you want to know where God stands on the issue? Don't miss this week!

Prayer focus for this week

Q: The Question — *What is the writer saying?*
A: The Answer — *How Can I apply this to my life?*

Sunday • Matthew 16:1-12

DIGGING DEEPER • There may be nothing more enjoyable to eat than freshly baked bread soaked in butter. In baking the bread, the yeast is very important. If there is too much yeast, the bread will overflow the pan and be no good. On the other hand, if there is not enough yeast, then the bread will not rise and is ruined. It is not enough that you have yeast, but that you have the right amount. Jesus told the disciples the importance of yeast. In the Bible, yeast is a symbol of sin, and here the sin is false doctrine. Doctrine is important to the Christian life; however, the right doctrine makes all the difference. That is why Satan works hard to change or delete doctrine in your life. Wrong doctrine produces wrong principles. **Doctrine is as important to your Christian walk as yeast is to bread. Do not allow Satan to downplay the importance of doctrine in your life.**

Monday • Matthew 16:13-23

Q & A

DIGGING DEEPER • Playing 20 Questions is a lot of fun; some make it even more challenging by changing it to 10 Questions. It is fun to try to figure out what someone else is thinking. In today's passage, Jesus changed 20 Questions to two questions. His first question was, "Who do people say I am?" The disciples answered, "John the Baptist, Elias, Jeremias, or one of the prophets." Then Jesus asked the disciples who they thought he was. Peter stepped up and said, "Thou art the Christ, the Son of the living God." Jesus told the disciples that Peter was right, and the fact that Jesus was the Messiah is what the church will be built on. This is the first mention of the church in the New Testament.
Who is Jesus to you? Teachers of false doctrine do not believe that Jesus is the only Son of God and Savior of the world. Their yeast (sin) is showing.

Tuesday • Matthew 16:24-17:13

Q & A

DIGGING DEEPER • There are people who give up everything they have to follow a false religion. In today's passage, Jesus told the disciples that those who follow Him must take up their cross to do so. Taking up their cross meant to be willing to suffer through any kind of treatment the world is willing to hand out to the followers of Christ. Those who follow Christ must not expect any better treatment from the world than Jesus received. Jesus then took Peter, James, and John up a mountain to show them the glory to come. They saw Jesus in all His glory along with Moses, and Elias. The life to come will be worth any mistreatment we receive on this earth.
Jesus never promised an easy life for His followers. The question is, "Are you willing to suffer for Jesus now to enjoy a greater life later?"

Wednesday • Matthew 17:14-27

Q&A

DIGGING DEEPER • Skydiving takes a lot of faith. Once you jump out of the plane, there is nothing to keep you from dying except for that small white parachute. Now, you can talk about how great that parachute works, but until you jump out of the plane, it does not mean a thing. Jesus told the disciples they could not cure a sick child – not because of their little faith, but because they had no faith at all! Ouch, that must have hurt. To be told you have little faith is one thing, but to be told you have no faith really makes you mad. Many times we do not see God working in our lives, not because we have little faith, but because we have no faith at all. What are you trusting God to do?
How would God respond to your faith today? Is your faith small, or do you have any faith at all? Ask God to help you believe His Word.

Thursday • Matthew 18:1-20

Q&A

DIGGING DEEPER • We live in a world where people are easily offended by what we say or do. Many times we tend to overlook these offenses, because we feel we have the right to do whatever we want. Jesus told the disciples that offending people is a very serious problem. Jesus gave a pattern to follow when offenses take place. The one offended is to go to the one who offends. This allows them to make things right and keep a friendship. Many times the person offended never goes to the offender. Instead he allows bitterness to build up in his life, which affects his relationships with others, even his relationship with God. If you are offended, go to the offender; if you have offended, then ask for forgiveness. No excuses.
Offending people is not something in which we should take pleasure. Jesus was very careful not to offend even when rejected. Are you careful?

Friday • Matthew 18:21-35

DIGGING DEEPER • Many families stare destruction in the face because pride does not allow family members to forgive each other. On the heels of yesterday, Peter asked Jesus how many times he must be expected to forgive someone. Jesus told Peter 490 times! Now, this was not so Peter could keep count. The idea Jesus gives is that it is not the amount of forgiveness but the act of forgiveness that should concern us. Jesus' example is to show that He takes forgiveness, or the lack of it, very seriously. When you are a forgiving person, you have very little patience for those who refuse to forgive.
Is the Holy Spirit bringing to your mind someone whom you need to forgive? Remember how much Jesus forgave you! Start right now by forgiving someone who has mistreated you this week.

Saturday • Matthew 19:1-15

DIGGING DEEPER • Today, young people face the issue of divorce more than any other time in history. Statistics show there are more divorces among Christian couples than non-Christian couples. In today's passage, the Pharisees tried to trick Jesus with their questions about divorce. They believed, according to Moses, a man could divorce his wife just because she did not please him. Jesus set them straight by showing them Moses' consent to divorce was given because of the people's hard hearts, not because it was okay with God. In God's plan, a man and a woman were to stay married until one of them died. That is still God's plan, and that is why marriage is a very serious matter.
Marriage is not something two people try out for a while to see if it works. Is marriage as serious to you as it is to God? It should be. It is for life.

qt WEEK 23

This week Matthew spends a lot of time helping us understand that the way we think is very important. Every person is developing a grid work (his mind) through which every thought will be filtered. This grid work is important, so be careful whom you are allowing to structure yours. This week will cause you to think!

Prayer focus for this week

Q: The Question — *What is the writer saying?*
A: The Answer — *How Can I apply this to my life?*

Sunday • Matthew 19:16-30

DIGGING DEEPER • When you have a responsibility to fulfill, it is great to have a checklist so that you can mark the items off as you do them; that way you know when you are done. In today's passage, a young, rich man approached Jesus and desired such a list for his entrance into heaven. Jesus was kind enough to oblige the young man with a shortened list of the Ten Commandments. Instead of convicting this young man, the list made him feel pretty good about himself. Jesus then proceeded to the important aspect by telling the young man to sell everything he had and then follow Him. Because of the man's greedy heart, he could not bring himself to part with his material goods. Poor choice… even worse consequences! **Earthly wealth is no ticket to heaven. The world drives us to be greedy, especially with money. A repentant heart, not money, gets one into heaven.**

Monday • Matthew 20:1-16

DIGGING DEEPER • Have you ever had a job where you felt you were doing most of the work while others were being paid most of the money? Today Jesus deals with this attitude. In this passage, the landowner went out and hired people to work all day for a penny. He went out three other times during the day and hired three more groups of people to work without giving an amount to be paid. When the day was done, the landowner paid the last group of workers the same amount of money as he paid the first group of workers who had worked all day, even though the last group had worked just a portion of the day. Some are saved at an early age while others are saved later on in life. They both get to enjoy the benefits of heaven! **If you were saved early in life, rejoice. You have many years to serve the Lord and earn rewards; whereas, someone older has only a few years.**

Tuesday • Matthew 20:17-34

DIGGING DEEPER • Everyone wants to be the man or woman on top – the person who gets all the benefits, the person everyone else serves. Even the disciples were caught up in this mind-set. James and John, along with their mother, came to Jesus to ask to be allowed to sit on the right hand and left hand of Jesus in His kingdom. These two seats are right next to the top man; these two seats have power, prestige, honor, and fame. Jesus told them that greatness in the kingdom of God comes in the form of servanthood. Those who would hold the highest places in the kingdom would be those who served others. This lesson in humility must have been very hard for the disciples to understand.
In our world, servants are not leaders; however, in the kingdom of God, servants are the greatest leaders. How is your servanthood today?

Wednesday • Matthew 21:1-22

Q&A

DIGGING DEEPER • Have you ever had someone sing your praises one day, then turn around a few days later and accuse you of doing wrong? This is a terrible feeling, and one that Jesus felt also. In today's passage, Jesus entered Jerusalem while the people all around were singing His praises, calling Him "Lord". In just a few days, these very people would be standing before Pilate crying out for Jesus to be crucified. The fig tree in today's passage is a picture of this superficial worship. While the tree looked good, it produced no fruit. In the same manner, many people worship Jesus outwardly in order to look good, but they are empty on the inside. True worship of God comes from the heart, not the outward acts people perform. **True worship comes from within the heart of a person. Hypocrisy makes God sick, just as it makes us sick. Make sure your worship is true.**

Thursday • Matthew 21:23-46

Q&A

DIGGING DEEPER • Have you ever been in a room that was so dark you could not see your hand in front of your face? It is rather scary. Then finally some light comes into the room, and you are so glad to see it. This is a great picture of the world. The people in the world are walking around in pitch darkness, scared, looking for some kind of light. In today's passage, Jesus told the Jews that He is giving the light to the church, and they are to be responsible for sharing it with the world. The church will never take the place of the Jews; however, the church will have a place beside the Jews in the kingdom of God. Every person that is part of the church has a responsibility to shine forth Jesus' light in his corner of the world. **God has given you the light of the Gospel and the responsibility to share this light. Are you fulfilling your responsibility?**

Friday • Matthew 22:1-14

DIGGING DEEPER • How would you feel if you had a birthday party and invited all your friends, then no one showed up? Well, that is exactly how the king in today's passage felt. All of his friends turned him down, so he destroyed them all and sent out an invitation to anyone who would like to come. Many came and received a white robe; however, one came who did not want a robe. It seemed this man wanted to come on his own terms. The king had him cast out, never to enjoy his hospitality. Jesus offered the Jews a kingdom; they rejected it, so Jesus destroyed them and opened His offer to the Gentiles. Those who come must have a white robe (a picture of Jesus' righteousness); those without a robe will be cast out. **Jesus' offer of salvation is to everyone who wants to accept. At the same time, no one can come to Jesus on his own terms. Got your robe?**

Saturday • Matthew 22:15-33

DIGGING DEEPER • Have you ever had someone try to trick you into saying something wrong? Today two groups come to Jesus and try to trick him into saying something they could hold against him. First, the Herodians asked Jesus about paying tribute. Jesus told them to give to Caesar those things that belong to Caesar, and give to God those things that belong to God. The second group were the Sadducees (this was one of the religious leader groups), who did not believe in the Resurrection. They posed a hypothetical question (don't you just love these questions?) about marriage and the afterlife. Jesus embarrassed them by telling them they did not know their doctrine.
Satan will always try to trap you with the Bible; that is why it is important for you to know the doctrines in God's Word. Get ready for Satan's traps.

qt WEEK 24

This week the Holy Spirit is going to talk to you about cleaning up your life, making sure you are on the inside what you claim to be on the outside. The Holy Spirit will show you why it is important to clean up your life everyday; you never know what a day will bring.

Prayer focus for this week

Q: The Question — *What is the writer saying?*
A: The Answer — *How Can I apply this to my life?*

Sunday • Matthew 22:34-46

DIGGING DEEPER • Today's passage is the conclusion to last week's attempt to trap Jesus with words. After hearing that Jesus closed the mouths of the Herodians and embarrassed the Sadducees, the Pharisees felt like it was their turn to show the others how it was done. The Pharisees posed a question about the greatest commandment, which Jesus answered was to love God, while the second greatest was to love your neighbor. Then Jesus turned the tables by asking them a question: If David called Jesus "Lord", then how can Jesus be David's son? With no answer to give, the Pharisees knew they were done. After this, these groups decided it was not such a good idea to try to trap Jesus with His words.

We are told to be ready with an answer of why we believe what we do, but it takes time spent in the Word of God. Are you ready to learn?

Monday • Matthew 23:1-12

Q&A

DIGGING DEEPER • We live in a world where titles are important. People want titles more than they want jobs. Titles tend to make people feel important. In Jesus' day, things were not much different. The Pharisees and Sadducees liked their titles and the privileges that came with them. These religious leaders were not concerned with helping the people; they were concerned with looking good when in public. Jesus told the common people to beware these religious leaders, because their teachings were not helping them move closer to God. Titles are not always important, as they can become a burden. Instead of living to impress people, God's children should be living to please their heavenly Father.
Titles do not make men, and they certainly do not make spiritual men. Are you living to earn a title, or are you living to please your heavenly Father?

Tuesday • Matthew 23:13-26

Q&A

DIGGING DEEPER • How many of us would eat out of a dirty bowl? Have you ever looked at a bowl, thought "this is a clean bowl," and then looked on the inside only to find it dirty with old, dried on food? Jesus told the religious leaders that they are like dishes that look clean on the outside, but on the inside are nasty. Jesus told these groups that they are the worst of all. Not only are they headed down the road to hell, but they are leading people down the same road. Jesus said they put on a great act, but that is all it is – an act. There is not one ounce of godliness in how they lived. It is easy to fool people by the way we live; however, God is able to look on the inside, and He knows who we really are.
Are you an actor (hypocrite) in your Christian life? Are you just fooling people so they will like you? You cannot fool God; He knows you!

Wednesday • Matthew 23:27-39

DIGGING DEEPER • Today many people dislike politicians because they make many promises to the public in order to be elected, then, after their election, they seldom keep their promises. Sometimes religious people act just like politicians by claiming to act a certain way, but in reality, they live just the opposite. In today's section, Jesus finished his woes upon the Jewish nation for their rejection of the Messiah. This last woe tells them they will be put aside for their rejection and be held responsible for the death of the prophets God sent them, just as their fathers were before them. This is also a warning to others that a hollow Christian life is useless and considered a terrible thing before God.
If you are going to talk the talk, then walk the walk. Do not become one of those people upon whom Jesus pronounced woes. Live what you talk!

Thursday • Matthew 24:1-14

DIGGING DEEPER • Have you ever wondered what the future will be like? The disciples were no different. In today's passage, Jesus told the disciples that the temple they were so proud of would one day be destroyed. This caught the attention of the disciples, and they assumed that when the temple was destroyed, it would be the sign that Jesus was coming to set up the kingdom they were looking for. However, Jesus began to tell them about the Tribulation period, where many people will be killed because of their faith. In addition, false prophets who claim to be Christ will deceive many people. During this time, the Gospel of the kingdom will be preached.
We are many days closer to the days of the Tribulation period. It is time for us to be faithful in sharing the good news of salvation to the world.

Friday • Matthew 24:15-31

DIGGING DEEPER • Don't you hate it when you are watching a movie and someone gives away the ending? Well, that is what Jesus did in this section. He began to tell the disciples what the end of time will be like. The Tribulation period will be the worst time ever in the history of the world, and there will be many who will come saying they are Christ. However, when Christ comes back, it will not be a secret; it will be such a big event that no one will have to be told He is back. The neat thing is that when Jesus comes back, the church will come back with Him. Now is the time to get on the right side of this event. This is the time to make sure you are part of the church; once the church is gone, it is too late to change your mind. **As a child of God, you know how the story turns out. Now is the time to tell everyone you know, so they are not surprised when Jesus returns.**

Saturday • Matthew 24:32-51

DIGGING DEEPER • How does Mom act when the family knows company is coming? Most moms go into cleaning overload; they clean the house better than ever, and expect everybody in the house to have the same attitude. Why does Mom go crazy when company is coming? She wants her house to be spotless for the company. Many Christians are living as if they will have time to clean up before Jesus comes; however, there will be no notice of His return. When Jesus comes, it will be like company showing up on the front porch without any notice – everything will be just like it is every day. There will be no time for cleaning up, so anything that needs to be cleaned up must be cleaned up now while there is still time. **God the Father knows when Jesus will return. If Jesus came back today, would you be surprised? Any changes need to be made today!**

WEEK 25

Matthew covers several aspects of the Christian life this week. He talks about the seriousness of faking it. He also deals with the importance of believers keeping up their responsibilities of faithfulness, and supporting the nation of Israel. He then touches on our prayer life, and reminds us of what Jesus has done for us.

Prayer focus for this week

Q: The Question — *What is the writer saying?*
A: The Answer — *How Can I apply this to my life?*

Sunday • Matthew 25:1-13

DIGGING DEEPER • Have you ever been waiting at home for a package to come in the mail? You wait all day, then something comes up and you have to leave to take care of it. While you are gone, the carrier comes with your package, but he cannot leave it; instead, he leaves a slip of paper telling you he came while you were gone. In today's passage, we read about ten virgins who were waiting for their groom to come and get them. Five of the virgins did not have oil for their lamps, so they had to go into town to buy some. While they were gone, the groom came and left them behind. This is of course a parable for the Jews; however, the church is waiting for Jesus to return and must be ready when He comes.

Those who are faking a relationship with Christ will be left behind when Jesus comes for the church. Is your relationship real?

Monday • Matthew 25:14-30

DIGGING DEEPER • There are people who attempt to do things even though great risk is involved. Sometimes they fail and other times they succeed. Success comes because they take a chance. Today's lesson has to deal with faith. There are some Christians who step out in faith to do things for God – some small, some not so small. The size of the project is not what matters; the faith involved to step out is what matters. Each man who acts according to the measure of faith with which he has been entrusted is commended and rewarded at the return of his lord. The wicked servant does nothing with the faith he is given, and therefore is unprepared when his lord returns. Because he is unbelieving, he is rejected.
We cannot force someone to accept God's offer of salvation (that is not our job). However, our job is to bring the Gospel to every person we can.

Tuesday • Matthew 25:31-46

DIGGING DEEPER • Just saying you love someone is very shallow. The depth of your love is shown when you do things for them no matter what the cost. As Jesus finished His discourse here in chapter 25, He gave a prophetic story. After His return, He will sit in the seat of judgment and divide the sheep (believers) from the goats (unbelievers). Their belief or unbelief will be seen in how they treated the nation of Israel. True followers of God will love and care for His chosen people, the Jews, while those who hate God will also hate the Jews. This is why it is important for America to show favor toward the Jews. God blesses those who care for His children.
With all the hype about the Middle East today, how important do you feel it is that we support the Jewish nation of Israel?

Wednesday • Matthew 26:1-16

Q&A

DIGGING DEEPER • Many teenagers and adults play on sports teams, in bands, go to school, and work jobs where they give it everything they have to be the best. Now there is nothing wrong with giving your all; however, when it comes to living for Christ, giving our all is not always what God gets. In today's passage, Mary came to Jesus with a box of ointment – oil that cost a year's wages – and poured it over Jesus' head. The disciples under the leadership of Judas began to complain saying that this was a waste. Mary was giving everything she had to Jesus, and that is never a waste.

The world thinks Christians are foolish for giving everything to God. God, on the other hand, knows we are foolish for giving everything to the world. Who would you rather have thinking you are foolish?

Thursday • Matthew 26:17-29

Q&A

DIGGING DEEPER • When someone in the immediate family comes down with a type of life-threatening illness, most people would tell the doctors to spare no expense in finding a cure. Why? Because we love that person and do not want to lose them. In today's passage we are reminded how much Jesus gave to save us from our death sentence of sin. Each time we partake of the Lord's Supper, we are to reflect on what Jesus gave up and went through to redeem us from our hopeless state of sin and death. Since Jesus was willing to give up so much for us, why do we find it so hard to surrender our will and give our best to Him?

While you may not be taking communion at your church this week, it is still a great idea to stop and remember what Jesus has done for you.

Friday • Matthew 26:30-46

DIGGING DEEPER • A consistent prayer life may be the hardest thing a Christian tries to develop. Why is it so hard to pray? In our passage today, Jesus told the disciples their flesh, not their lack of commitment, was the reason they had a hard time praying. In the Garden of Gethsemane Jesus earnestly prayed to His Father. Notice the progression of Jesus' prayer: First, He prayed for the cup to pass. Next, He prayed for God's will to be done. Thirdly, He prayed the same as the second prayer with an attitude of submission. How often do we pray for our will instead of God's will? In your prayer time, ask God to make His will known to you.
Prayer is something we talk about; however, many of us would not consider ourselves to be prayer warriors. Today, let's increase our efforts.

Saturday • Matthew 26:47-56

DIGGING DEEPER • Many people reject the idea of speaking out for Jesus in public because it might embarrass them. In today's passage, we see Jesus standing in the face of humiliation for those He loved. Judas brought the chief priests and Roman guards to the garden where Jesus was praying. He then proceeded to betray Jesus with the kiss of a friend, a symbol of love. Jesus even called him friend. After the shocking incident of Peter cutting off the servant's ear, Jesus offered no resistance. He was not forced to surrender by any earthly power; He was freely giving Himself up. Jesus willingly suffered the humiliation of an arrest and His friends bailing out on Him, because He loved us.
Jesus was willing to suffer much humiliation for us. Is it really so hard to suffer some small amount of humiliation to tell others about His love?

WEEK 26

This week you will learn what peer pressure is all about, and how to deal with compromising. You will also learn how to show true love to others, how many ways there are to heaven, and what responsibility God has left you to accomplish. This week the Holy Spirit will stretch you to your very limits.

Prayer focus for this week

Q: The Question — *What is the writer saying?*
A: The Answer — *How Can I apply this to my life?*

Sunday • Matthew 26:57-75

DIGGING DEEPER • Peer pressure sometimes causes us to go backward when we intend to go forward. In today's passage, Peter, who may have been accompanied by a few of the other disciples, watched as Jesus was questioned by the Roman authorities and falsely accused by the Jewish leaders. They spit on Him and beat Him, then He was mocked by the Roman soldiers and led away to be abused some more. One in the group outside recognized Peter and announced to the crowd that Peter was a follower of Christ. Peter denied that he knew the Lord, even swearing to make his point. Suddenly, a rooster crowed and Peter was reminded of his promise never to deny Him. How awful Peter must have felt!
Peer pressure is stronger than most people even think. Ask the Holy Spirit to help you overcome the peer pressure you are facing today.

Monday • Matthew 27:1-14

DIGGING DEEPER • One of the neatest things about acting is that we can dress up and act like someone we are not on the inside. We may fool many people; but we never fool ourselves. This type of acting is fun and entertaining; however, there are people who act or pretend to be followers of Christ. This type of acting is not fun at all. Today we read about Judas, who followed Christ around for three years, yet when it came down to it, he really did not believe in Christ. Judas could not fool himself, and the guilt became so unbearable that he committed suicide. Judas shows us that it is not enough to know who Jesus is. Salvation comes through an acceptance of Jesus Christ as the one and only Son of God who died for you.
Many people can be fooled by the way we act; however, there are two people we never fool: God and ourselves. Is your Christianity for real?

Tuesday • Matthew 27:15-32

DIGGING DEEPER • Can you think of any time in your life when you had to compromise to make things work out? Compromising is not always a bad thing. In our passage today, we see an example of compromising that is not good. Pilate wanted to let Jesus go, but the Jewish crowd was crying out for Jesus' death. Pilate even gave them a way out by having them choose whom to set free – Jesus or Barabbas. This was actually Pilate's way out. Pilate was taken aback when the crowd chose the criminal, Barabbas. Pilate knew Jesus was innocent; however, he also knew if he displeased the Jewish crowd it could cost him his job. Instead of taking the right stand, Pilate compromised to save his job; however, he may have lost his soul!
Satan will always present the opportunity for you to compromise your beliefs. Know what the Bible teaches and stick to your beliefs.

Wednesday • Matthew 27:33-50

Q&A

DIGGING DEEPER • What is real love? In our world people say that true love is sex; however, if that is true, then there would be fewer divorces. In today's passage, we see a wonderful picture of what true love is all about. The Roman soldiers took Jesus to Golgotha where they performed the most brutal of all deaths. Crucifixion was a terrible way to die. As you read today, do not just quickly read the passage; slow down and think about what you are reading. Think about what Jesus went through to pay for your sins. True love is the willingness to sacrifice for others. Jesus gave the ultimate sacrifice, His life, to prove how much He loves you.

It is easier to tell people you love them than to show it. This week, do more than talk about love; show the people in your life how much you love them.

Thursday • Matthew 27:51-66

Q&A

DIGGING DEEPER • Sam's Club is a giant warehouse of goods for sale; however, to buy something from Sam's Club a person must be a member. When you go to the store, there is a sign hanging on the door that says "Members Only." While heaven does not have any signs hanging on the door, there is only one way to get in. In our passage today, we read about the death of Jesus Christ and the events that took place. One of those events was the splitting of the temple veil from top to bottom. Now everyone has access to God. However, there is only one way a person will get into heaven. Only those who have accepted Jesus' work on the cross as payment for their sin will be allowed into heaven.

It is said that "all roads lead to Rome"; however, not all roads lead to Heaven. Make sure you are on the right road, and then tell others about it.

Friday • Matthew 28:1-10

DIGGING DEEPER • We have read several times in the last ten weeks where Jesus told his disciples that He would die and three days later rise from the dead. In today's passage, that is exactly what happens. After Jesus' death, He is taken off the cross, wrapped in white linen, and then placed in a new grave. Three days later, Mary and her friends come to put oil on the body of Jesus. When they arrive at the gravesite there are two angels sitting on the stone next to the open grave. They tell the ladies that Jesus is not in the grave – He has risen, just as He said He would. They are shocked; after all, no one has ever risen before. The angels then tell the ladies to go and tell the disciples that Jesus is alive.
Jesus keeps His word. He said He would rise again, and He did. He promises you a home in heaven if you are a believer. It will happen!

Saturday • Matthew 28:11-20

DIGGING DEEPER • How many times have your parents given you instructions about things they wanted done while they were gone? Have you ever waited until the last minute to accomplish the task? If you have, you've probably been caught with the work not done. In the last few verses of Matthew 28, Jesus is about to leave, so He gives His followers the task of making disciples everywhere they go. This task has been passed on down to us today. We are to make disciples everywhere we go. The question is not "is Jesus coming back," but rather, "when Jesus comes back, will He find you still working at the task"?
God expects His children to complete their tasks. What are you doing to make disciples where you are?

qt WEEK 27

Do you need wisdom? Have you ever been tempted and did not know how to keep from failing? Have you ever just not fit in? Do you think others are not good enough for you? Have you ever found a contradiction in Scripture? Have you ever said something you wish you could take back? If so, this week is for you!

Prayer focus for this week

Q: The Question — *What is the writer saying?*
A: The Answer — *How Can I apply this to my life?*

Sunday • James 1:1-8

DIGGING DEEPER • As you walk into math class, you see a strange sight. All of your friends are actually studying. "Dude, did you watch the game last night?," you ask. As your best friend totally ignores you, a sickening feeling comes to your stomach. That's right! The big test is today and you are not prepared. As James writes to Jewish Christians scattered all over the world, he reminds us that the tests and trials that we face in life should not make us queasy, but bring about joy. Joy… because tests bring patience and patience brings completeness or maturity. However, if we do lack wisdom, we should ask God to give us the wisdom we need, believing that He will provide.

What kinds of tests are you facing today? How can you be joyful in those tests? In what area do you need God's wisdom today?

Monday • James 1:9-18

DIGGING DEEPER • Have you ever had an opinion about someone with no solid basis for it? Maybe you have decided that the new, quiet girl is a snob because she hasn't talked to you yet. Perhaps you think the star football player is mentally subpar because he is, well, a football player. Many people have pre-judged God this way. "Since God is all-powerful, he could have stopped that temptation from coming into my life." James reminds us that God does not try to get us to sin. He may test us with difficulties in our lives, but He never tempts us to sin. Our own sinful lusts and desires are the source of temptation. God is the giver of good and perfect gifts (v. 17), not temptation (v. 13). God promises a crown for everyone who endures temptation without falling.
How will you yield your desires to Christ this week when you are tempted?

Tuesday • James 1:19-27

DIGGING DEEPER • Beep. Beep. Beep. The alarm goes off for the fifth time as you finally crawl out of bed. You stumble to the bathroom picking sleepy dirt out of your eyes. You take one look in the mirror, grab your backpack and head off to school. Right? Of course not… that would be social suicide. James reminds us that the Word of God is like a mirror for our souls. It shows us where we need work. If we do not act upon what the Bible reveals about our lives, it is like getting out of bed and going straight to school. We are reminded to listen to and linger in the Word (v. 19, 25), lose our wicked ways (v. 21), lasso our own words (v. 26), labour among the widows (v. 27), and leave the way of the world (v. 27).
What does the Bible show you concerning your soul? What changes will you make today as a result of looking into God's Word?

Wednesday • James 2:1-9

DIGGING DEEPER • In every high school cafeteria you will find a reoccurring phenomenon. Each table has a label. The jocks sit in one area, the nerds in another, the mean girls sit somewhere close to the jocks, and the losers sit in the back corner. How dare a computer geek guy think he has the right to sit with the cheerleaders! In James' day it wasn't taking place in a cafeteria, but in the church. He clearly reminds us not to play favorites (have respect of persons). He plainly says that loving your neighbor is good (v. 8), but having respect of persons is sin (v. 9). You are not better than anyone else, regardless of your social status or wealth. Live like a Christian, but do it without playing favorites (v. 1).
How can you show the love of Christ to someone outside of your normal group of friends? Today, try loving your neighbor as yourself.

Thursday • James 2:10-18

DIGGING DEEPER • Have you ever met someone who was prone to making up stories? You know, he is the guy who swears that he talked with LeBron James, the NBA player, last night at Wal-Mart. Maybe it is the girl who shook hands with that famous movie star. It is easy to smirk in unbelief until he pulls out the LeBron autograph, or she whips out that picture of herself with "what's his name." James sports the same smirk of unbelief toward people who say they are Christians, but do not live like it. Just like that claim of a LeBron visit is suspect without the autograph, so are our claims of faith without works. If you claim to have saving faith, prove your faith with your actions. Works will not produce faith, but real faith works.
How can you show your faith this week by your good works? In what Christian Service can you participate this week?

Friday • James 2:19-26

DIGGING DEEPER • Did you read verse 21? Did it not just say that Abraham was justified by works? Wait a minute! The Bible also says, "For by grace are ye saved through faith…not of works" (Ephesians 2:8-9). What is going on here? Is the Bible contradicting itself? No Way! Here is the truth: As James is writing about Abraham, he discusses two different time periods of his life. In Genesis 15, Abraham was considered "righteous" by believing God. In Genesis 22, he proved his faith by his works. Faith and works go together. If you are truly saved, if you truly have faith, you will prove your faith with your actions. Others cannot tell you are a Christian unless you do something to prove it.
What can you do today? How will you show the world that you have faith in Jesus Christ?

Saturday • James 3:1-10

DIGGING DEEPER • There is power in small things. The bit is used to turn a horse (v. 3). The helm is used to steer a gigantic ship (v. 4). The spark can ignite a fire that could destroy the largest forest (v. 5). And then there is the tongue…just a small member of your body but with such potential for destruction (vv. 5-6). The same tongue that praises the Lord often curses man. It is almost as if you can see the Apostle James shaking his head as he writes, "My brethren, these things ought not so to be" (v. 10). James reminds us that if we can just get control of our tongues, we are very mature and capable of controlling the rest of our bodies (v. 2).
How will you control your tongue today? What can you do to stop yourself from using your tongue as a destructive force? Will you commit to pray before you speak?

qt WEEK 28

Did you ever want someone to tell you exactly what to do? If you could just get specific instructions, your life would be a lot easier. Well, this is your week. James gives specific instructions on how to use your time and money, how to be patient, how to be wise, and how to pray. It is simple. Just read and apply.

Prayer focus for this week

Q: The Question *What is the writer saying?*
A: The Answer *How Can I apply this to my life?*

Sunday • James 3:11-18

DIGGING DEEPER • Who is the wisest person in your class? Just how wise is your teacher? The world likes to pour out applause on those who are academically intelligent. However, the Bible sees wisdom differently. The Apostle James says that a wise man should perform good works in meekness (v. 13). He also defines heavenly wisdom as "pure, then peaceable, gentle, and easy to be intreated, full of mercy and good fruits, without partiality, and without hypocrisy" (v. 17). In contrast, the wisdom of the world produces "bitter envying and strife," a puffed up attitude, and deceitfulness (v. 14). So, which do you have? We were told in chapter 1 to ask for wisdom if we needed it. What type of wisdom do you want?
How can you obtain the wisdom of God? How will you make God's wisdom a priority in your life this week?

Monday • James 4:1-5

Q
A

DIGGING DEEPER • Do you believe in Santa Claus? Yeah, when we were a kid and wanted something. But all too often that is how we treat God. "Hey, God, could you give me a…". Maybe you take the more spiritual approach, "Our Great and Heavenly Father, wilt Thou please give me a…". Sounds funny, right? In James 4, the people were not getting their prayers answered. James told them that they were asking God for their desires with a selfish motive (v. 3). The people were fighting among themselves, and James reminded them that disunity comes as a result of their own lusts. Because of their selfish give-me and me-first attitudes, and their friendships with the world, the people were having problems with each other.
How will your prayer life change today as a result of seeing this negative example? Try praying today without asking God for anything.

Tuesday • James 4:6-10

Q
A

DIGGING DEEPER • Sometimes the Scripture is very easy to apply to everyday living. In today's passage, James is pretty specific and practical. 1. Be humble because God "resisteth (opposes) the proud, but giveth grace to the humble." 2. Be submissive to God and resist the devil and Satan will have to run. 3. Draw close to God and in turn He will draw close to you. 4. Clean up spiritually and be sad about the sin you have allowed to creep into your life. 5. Humble yourself in God's eyes and He will lift you up.
What can you do today to practice humility? How can you be submissive to God today? In what area will you resist the devil? What action can you take that will draw you closer to God? Will you weep over the sin in your life today? What steps will you take today to remove that sin?

Wednesday • James 4:11-17

DIGGING DEEPER • What do you have planned for tomorrow? For next month? What about a year from now? If you are like most of us, you just take for granted that the plans that you make will happen. The Apostle James, however, warns of boasting about the future. He reminds us that life is short and God has ultimate control over what you will do. Since life is like a vapor (mist) (v. 14), James reminds us to speak lovingly toward our brothers in Christ, and remember that God is the only judge (vv. 11-12). In verse 17, James reminds us that if we know that we should do something good and fail to do it, we are sinning. Whether it is driving the speed limit or cleaning our rooms, we should simply do what we know is right. **Will you surrender your future to God? In what area do you need to decide to simply do right? Toward whom will you begin to speak lovingly?**

Thursday • James 5:1-6

DIGGING DEEPER • Some students have bought into the get rich or die tryin' mentality that the world promotes. Oh, you may say, "This passage is talking to rich people and I'm not rich." James reminds all of us that hoarding money will do us no good. He gets specific by condemning the action of accumulating money at the expense of others (v. 4). He rebukes the mentality of living in pleasure on earth by condemning and killing the just (vv. 5-6). Yes, it is easy to condemn the rich for these actions, but you do not have to be rich to sin in this way. The sin of obtaining money at the expense of others is not limited to the wealthy. You can be poor and love money. Your focus must not be about money.
How can you avoid an unbiblical focus on money? What will you do this week to keep your focus on Christ?

Friday • James 5:7-12

DIGGING DEEPER • "I just can't wait until school's out." "I can't wait until this weekend." "I'm starving! I can't wait until dinner… I gotta eat something now." Have you ever said something like that? Sure you have. Haven't we all? In today's passage, James focuses on patience. He lets us know that Jesus is coming back and that we should patiently wait for His return. By reminding us of the suffering of the prophets and the endurance of Job, he encourages us to live patiently. Finally, James commands us not to resort to taking oaths as proof of our honesty, but simply to say what we mean and mean what we say.
How can you be more patient this week as you wait for the return of Christ? How can the example of Job and other heroes of the faith encourage you?

Saturday • James 5:13-20

DIGGING DEEPER • Prayer is a powerful thing. If we have a physical problem, we should call for the elders of the church to pray. If we have a problem with a brother in Christ, we are to confess our faults and pray for each other. James reminds us that prayer is so powerful that when Elijah prayed for a drought, it did not rain for three and a half years! Prayer can change our lives. However, notice the stipulations on effective prayer. In verse 16, James says, "The effectual fervent prayer of a righteous man availeth much." Our prayers must be fervent, enthusiastic, avid, ardent, and impassioned. Secondly, our prayers to have any effect, we must be righteous.
Will you commit to following God's pattern for problem solving through prayer? What sin do you need to forsake in order for your prayers to be effective? Will you forsake it today?

WEEK 29

Do you know what God hates? Find out this week! What are you willing to do to gain wisdom in your life? Would you listen to your parents and stay away from immoral people? You'll see an unwise man and the consequences he faces, as well as the value of wisdom and ways to increase it in your life.

Prayer focus for this week

Q: The Question — *What is the writer saying?*
A: The Answer — *How Can I apply this to my life?*

Sunday • Proverbs 6:1-11

DIGGING DEEPER • Are you saying, "I'm not surety for anyone…I don't even know what that means"? A surety is someone who pledges to fulfill the obligations that another person makes. This goes beyond buying someone's lunch. This passage is warning us not to pledge to pay if others don't, and to get out of any such pledges if we have made them. On the other hand, we need to thank our Lord Jesus Christ for being our surety (Hebrews 7:22). He met the obligations to a holy God that we couldn't meet, by dying on the cross. Take a close look at the work the ant does. Each one does its individual job diligently and the whole colony is provided for. Get out of any surety that you're in. Thank the Lord for what He did for you. Are you doing the job God has for you to do? Check out Genesis 3:19 and 2 Thessalonians 3:10 for what God has to say about your job.

Monday • Proverbs 6:12-19

DIGGING DEEPER • Have you ever played a game and noticed someone cheating by motioning with his eyes or fingers to another person? It may have been in harmless fun, but wicked people who disregard the things of God take it to a deceitful evil level. Take a closer look again at the things God hates: Pride, lying, those who shed innocent blood, a heart that devises wicked imaginations/plans, feet that go to mischief/evil, a false witness, and those who sow discord/strife. Who would want anything in his life that God hates?
Is there even a little of something on that list in your life? Confess it as sin and turn to God to make positive changes in your life.

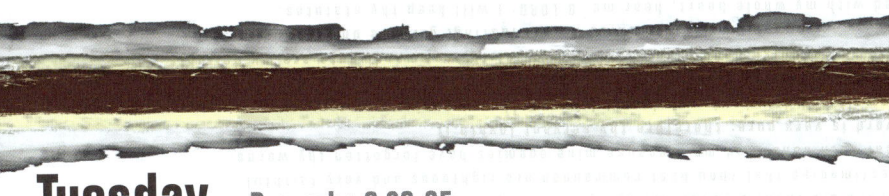

Tuesday • Proverbs 6:20-35

DIGGING DEEPER • Why should you listen to your parents? For most people, parents know and love you better than anyone else and only want what's best for you. They also remember their own youthful days and want you to learn from their instruction so as not to repeat some of the same mistakes. The rest of this passage deals with staying away from an evil or immoral woman. Sexual sin affects both the body and the soul of a person. It's not like stealing something that can be paid back. It's best to be forewarned of the consequences and determine now not to become a victim of such a person.
Thank your parents today for their love and concern for you. List the consequences found in this passage and determine what you will do if or when you are faced with a similar temptation.

Wednesday • Proverbs 7:1-9

Q&A

DIGGING DEEPER • Is it possible to really live and stay away from the trappings of evil people? Only if we obey God's commandments, desire His teaching, and seek wisdom and understanding. Then we will be able to control our actions by controlling our desires (Psalm 119:9-11). We see the willful steps of a young man who knew where he was going and foolishly chose to fall into the hands of an adulterous woman. He thought no one would see him going after dark. Even if no one did see him, God knew and was not pleased. God wants us to walk in His light as far away from darkness as possible – to seek His wisdom and understanding.
What commandments or teaching do you need to apply to your life? Look up Luke 11:35, John 8:12, and 1 Thessalonians 5:5 to decide what light you need in your life. What do you need to stay away from?

Thursday • Proverbs 7:10-18

Q&A

DIGGING DEEPER • When was the last time you had to go looking for trouble? Probably never – sin and evil have a way of finding us. Sin usually reveals itself to those who are discerning by its outward appearance, words, and actions. In today's passage the young man knew exactly what neighborhood he was in; plus she looked, sounded, and smelled just like a prostitute. That man thought he knew what he was doing. God had equipped him with eyes, ears, nose, and a free will to do what was right, but he chose to satisfy himself instead of what he knew God wanted him to do. Obviously, he was not thinking about what the consequences of his action might be. We'll see some of those tomorrow!
What does God want you to run away from? Read 2 Timothy 2:22 to find out. What does He want you to pursue before you are tempted?

Friday • Proverbs 7:19-27

DIGGING DEEPER • Think about what this young man is doing. He is dishonoring his parents (vv. 1-5). He is sinning against his neighbor (6:29), as well as his own soul (6:32). He is even sinning against his own body (1 Corinthians 6:16-18). Worst of all, he is sinning against a holy, righteous God (Genesis 39:9)! Look closely at the consequences he will face. He will be brought down (vv. 26-27) and will eventually die (Romans 6:23). The Bible tells us that a merciful God has provided one way out for a person who has fallen into sin. He must call on the Lord, confess his sin, and turn to a new life of obedience to God.
Look closely at your life and confess any sin that is separating you from the Lord. What consequences do you want to see in your life?

Saturday • Proverbs 8:1-11

DIGGING DEEPER • If you could ask for and receive anything you wanted, what would you ask for? Popularity? Money? The major theme of Proverbs is the superiority of wisdom and how we should desire it over anything else. Imagine craving wisdom over gold, silver, and jewels. Throughout Scripture the words knowledge, understanding, and wisdom are often linked together. Knowledge is the "input" of information to our mind. Understanding involves processing the information in our mind; and wisdom is using (output) the knowledge and understanding that we have processed.
What do you value more than wisdom? Wisdom is there waiting for you. Ask God to increase wisdom in your life (James 1:5).

qt WEEK 30

What does wisdom have to offer you? You'll find out a few things this week! You will be invited to a banquet by both wisdom and folly this week. Did you know there are consequences with either? Which one do you think you'd choose? You'll also learn how to tell the difference between a fool and a wise person.

Prayer focus for this week

Q: The Question — *What is the writer saying?*
A: The Answer — *How Can I apply this to my life?*

Sunday • Proverbs 8:12-21

DIGGING DEEPER • Do you want to be successful in life? What are you willing to do to become prosperous in the future? In this chapter, wisdom explains what she has to offer to those who seek her: understanding, truth, righteousness, instruction, and the ability to rule and judge. What happens to those who hate wisdom? They become wicked, perverse, and filled with evil, pride, and arrogance. With which list do you want to be associated? Good sense is a demonstration of wisdom. We need to remember that true treasure is spiritual rather than material. With wisdom you might receive material treasure as well, but it's not as important. **Confess any evil, pride, and arrogance in your life as sin. Ask God to give you wisdom! Is wisdom or material treasure more important to you?**

Monday • Proverbs 8:22-36

DIGGING DEEPER • How would you like to have been there to see the creation of the world? Can you imagine God and wisdom talking with each other about how high to make a certain mountain, or what color to make it, and how many petals to give different flowers? Isn't it comforting to know that God delights in wisdom and offers it to those who seek it? Wisdom is eternal and helps us make choices with eternity in mind, instead of what we think is right just for today or this week. All we have to do is listen to wisdom and blessings will come. There are rewards for those who pay attention to wisdom, and horrible consequences for those who fail to listen.
Will you pay attention to wisdom? What choices to you need to rethink with eternity in mind?

Tuesday • Proverbs 9:1-9

DIGGING DEEPER • What would you do if you were invited to a banquet at the White House with the President of the United States? That's not very likely, but your invitation to a banquet with wisdom is even better than that. In order to sit at wisdom's table, you must admit that you are simple. That doesn't mean you are mentally deficient – only that you lack wisdom and need (and want) assistance. The reward is to understand the way to life. How can you tell the difference between a wise person and a fool? Look at the way they respond to correction or criticism. The Biblical recipe for receiving more knowledge, wisdom, and faith is found in God's Word. The Holy Spirit will be your guide.
When was the last time you asked God for wisdom? Are you simple or wise? Test yourself by examining how you respond to correction.

Wednesday • Proverbs 9:10-18

DIGGING DEEPER • What do you do when you are invited to eat with someone? Sometimes there's not much to decide – you just go as you are. But other invitations require some preparation. For example, you'd dress differently when going out for pizza with friends than when going to a fancy wedding. Yesterday an invitation was given to you by wisdom. Today's invitation comes from folly. Why do so many feast at folly's table? Accepting her invitation requires no thought or work. It is the path of all who fail to choose wisdom. It is natural to place fleshly gratification over the well-being of the soul, and it'll cost for eternity. A disregard for God's plans and purposes will bring disaster to body and soul forever!
Do you fear the Lord? Which invitation are you accepting? Have you chosen to sit at wisdom's or folly's table?

Thursday • Proverbs 10:1-10

DIGGING DEEPER • As what kind of person do you want to be known and remembered? The book of Proverbs points out the extent to which our behavior affects others. A son makes his parents either glad or sad. By his behavior, he can bring blessed memories or sorrow. The book of Proverbs is in three main divisions: Starting in chapter ten, each verse teaches its own lesson mostly in the form of contrasting couplets. Most proverbs emphasize the positive effect of righteous behavior contrasted with the penalty for folly. How we use our hands affects our well-being (vv. 4-5). Verses 6-7 focus on our heads, while verse 9 speaks of the paths in which we direct our feet. All sin affects the well-being of others!
What would others say about you? Do you bring blessing or sorrow when you enter a room? Do something today to make your parents glad!

Friday • Proverbs 10:11-21

DIGGING DEEPER • Has someone ever hurt you with something they said, either to your face or behind your back? Probably! It could have been something careless or intentional, but it still hurts, doesn't it? Solomon takes seven of these eleven verses to talk about the mouth, tongue, or lips. That should get our attention! With that one little part of our body, we can do a lot of damage or a lot of good. It's your choice! One way Christians tend to misuse the tongue is by using words that are substitutes or slang for profanity. We should completely avoid common words that come from God's holy name.
Build up someone with your words today. Have you hurt someone with your tongue? Make it right. Determine to wipe Christian profanity from your vocabulary!

Saturday • Proverbs 10:22-32

DIGGING DEEPER • There are lots of promises in the Bible. Which ones do you cling to? When considering God's promises to the righteous, we must remember that in and of ourselves we possess no righteousness. It is only for those who have received the righteousness of Christ through repentance of sin. The righteous are promised answered prayer, eternal security, hope, gladness, the Lord's strength, wisdom, and discretion. On the other hand, the wicked are promised fear, shortened life, perished expectations, destruction, and loss of home and speech.
Do you have the righteousness of Christ? If not, ask for it today! Ask your leader to help. Which set of promises is true in your life?

qt WEEK 31

Any ordinary person can use a paint brush to paint a building or a hammer and chisel to carve away at something; but those same instruments in the hands of a master are used to create a masterpiece that is wonderful to behold. David was just such an instrument in God's hands, used to bring glory to Him.

Prayer focus for this week

Q: The Question — *What is the writer saying?*
A: The Answer — *How Can I apply this to my life?*

Sunday • 1 Chronicles 10:13-11:9

DIGGING DEEPER • Leaders are chosen every day around the world. Whether they lead nations, cities, or captain a team, people look to them for leadership and example. God removed King Saul from the throne of Israel by having him slain because he had ignored God's instructions. Although that may seem harsh, Saul had gone against God's instructions for years and would not turn back to Him. David had been the king of Judah for 7½ years before Saul was killed; now it was time to unite the kingdom. The people supported David as their leader because he led by example and showed courage when he took over the leadership of God's people.
Name two people you admire for their courage and leadership, and list why.
Name two young people you are influencing in the same way.

Monday • 1 Chronicles 11:10-19

DIGGING DEEPER • Every army has its best soldiers or warriors. These are the ones who are strong and courageous and won't quit when the battle gets tough. In today's passage, David's mighty men were willing to give their lives just to fulfill their king's desire for a drink of water. Behind the listing of their names is the thought that we are known by the company we keep. Just as important is the fact that we may be known by the leader we follow. The listing of these men and their exploits demonstrated that David was a leader who gained the full confidence and support of Israel's finest. These were the men who had received the Medal of Honor, so to speak, for service rendered to David and his kingdom.
Who are your heroes? Do you look for godly men and women who love the Lord, or just those who are the strongest and get the headlines?

Tuesday • 1 Chronicles 15:1-3; 25-29

DIGGING DEEPER • From the time we are little children we learn that we should obey those in authority. We also learn what to do and how to do it. These same principles have been in place for all of history. Here we have the account of David bringing the ark of the covenant to Jerusalem. This ark was the symbol of God's presence, promise, and blessing to His people, Israel. This was David's second attempt to move the ark. The first time he violated God's instruction by having it pulled on a cart rather than carried by men. This resulted in the death of Uzza, who reached out to steady the ark. David waited three months and reviewed God's instructions, and then followed them successfully, bringing the ark to Jerusalem.
List two laws that you believe are silly or wrong. Why do you obey or disobey these laws? Why is it important to obey God's laws?

Wednesday • 1 Chronicles 16:1-11

DIGGING DEEPER • We are all familiar with the celebration that follows a joyous occasion and the wonderful sense of satisfaction we have the following day. David led Israel in celebration before the Lord as the ark of the covenant entered the city, but then came the time to worship God and offer the praise and adoration due Him. Three key words in verse 4 provide a pattern for us: (1) to record–call to mind; (2) to thank–express gratitude to; and (3) to praise–celebrate the worth of (from which comes our word worship) their God. David closes with a psalm that contains as its core these great words: "Give thanks unto the LORD, call upon his name, make known his deeds among the people." Good instruction for us today!
List three things God has done for you lately. Thank Him for remembering you and for His act of love. Praise the Lord using David's pattern.

Thursday • 1 Chronicles 16:23-29

DIGGING DEEPER • Each of us wants to get better at something, and so we practice, take lessons, or have a tutor so we might improve. In today's passage, David gives instruction on how to worship the Lord and give Him praise. Here and in Psalm 96, David instructs his readers, and the whole earth, to sing unto the LORD. Singing is a natural way to praise the Lord. There are over seventy references to singing in the Psalms, many giving instructions to sing a new song. Doing so suggests that new mercies have been received, and the recipients are to daily announce his salvation, and declare his glory throughout the world. Learning to praise the Lord will help overcome a great deal of the negativity we face each day.
List two ways you can declare the glory of God to your friends and family. Talk to them, then write down how they respond to your testimony.

Friday • 1 Chronicles 17:1-15

DIGGING DEEPER • Remember when you thought of a good way to get something done, but Mom and Dad were able to help you do it even better? God said in Isaiah 55:8, "For my thoughts are not your thoughts, neither are your ways my ways," and that is illustrated here in today's passage. God had a better plan for building His house. The house that God would build was not to be made of earthly building materials. It would be a dynasty. God's plan was to choose a son of David to build His house, which would be known as the Temple. A parallel passage (2 Samuel 7:1-17) finds the author interested not only in the short-term implications of God's promise, but more importantly, in the Messiah (Christ) who will rule over God's eternal Kingdom.
Take time to surrender your plans to God and let Him give you better ones.

Saturday • 1 Chronicles 17:16-27

DIGGING DEEPER • Can you recall ever seeing a child who didn't get his way turn to his parent and say, "I agree with you, your way is best and I will do whatever you decide"? That would be very different than the normal crying fit we often see when Mom or Dad says "No." David's first response to God's promise, after God told him "No," was "Who am I, O LORD God, and what is mine house, that thou has brought me hitherto (this far)?" God at this point has brought him from shepherding to the palace, and now He is about to do even more. What God promised regarding the One to come was far beyond any of David's expectations, and he was keenly aware that its fulfillment was beyond his own powers.
List two times when God used you in people's lives to tell them of Christ or to be an encouragement to them.

qt WEEK 32

We understand the importance of a close relationship with our fathers; some of us because we have that privilege every day, and some because we don't get the time we want with Dad. Our Heavenly Father loves us and is always there. This week's passages show the proper response we should have toward God.

Prayer focus for this week

Q: The Question — *What is the writer saying?*
A: The Answer — *How Can I apply this to my life?*

Sunday • 1 Chronicles 21:18-26

DIGGING DEEPER • We hear people apologize all the time for crimes they have committed. True repentance, which is a change of heart and direction in life, is more than just saying "I'm sorry." Repentance includes a change in actions and attitude, and restitution (compensation), if necessary, to put things right. In David's day, animal sacrifices were made to God as evidence of a repentant heart. Two main points here: 1) David knew that forgiveness for sin costs something, and he would not accept for free Ornan's threshing floor and oxen, and 2) God accepted David's sacrifice as an act of repentance. Christ's death on the cross was the ultimate payment for our sin. He paid the price for our sin. It's paid in full! **This week, talk to someone who hasn't accepted Christ's payment for his sin and tell him about true repentance and the forgiveness it can bring.**

Monday • 1 Chronicles 22:1-10

DIGGING DEEPER • It is important as Christians to do all we can to serve the Lord no matter what our skills and abilities. David was not allowed to build the temple of the Lord because he was a man of blood. He had shed the blood of his enemies, making him unfit in God's plan to build the temple in which God would be worshiped. God's plan for David was to defend Israel from its enemies and unite the nation as one. God gave the responsibility of building the temple to David's son, Solomon. David's attitude was one of cooperation with God. Rather than complain because he didn't get his way, he prepared and collected all the materials so that Solomon could successfully build God's temple.
List two ways you can be a helper in a ministry at your church, even though you are not the one in charge.

Tuesday • 1 Chronicles 22:11-19

DIGGING DEEPER • David's charge to Solomon (father-to-son, king-to-successor) continues. His prayer to the Lord was that God would prosper Solomon as he undertook the building of God's house. He then asked that the Lord would give Solomon wisdom and understanding. This part of his fatherly advice was what encouraged the request for wisdom and knowledge that Solomon would later make of God (1 Kings 3:9; 2 Chronicles 1:10). David then challenged Solomon to "take heed to fulfill the statutes and judgments (ordinances) which the LORD charged Moses" with concerning Israel. This would bring blessing (success, prosperity) to Solomon and the people of Israel. Obedience always brings blessing.
List three times when you have been given good advice from your parents or others. Put them in order of most importance to your life.

Wednesday • 1 Chronicles 28:1-10

Q&A

DIGGING DEEPER • This is the account of David's desire to honor God by having Solomon build the temple. David encouraged Israel to recognize Solomon's leadership and to follow him in this magnificent effort to build the temple. He reviewed with them his original plan to build it himself, and how he had been disqualified by God because he was a warrior and not a man of peace. He announced that his son, a man of peace, would do the building. Solomon was qualified because he was David's chosen son, who himself had been chosen from the elect tribe of Judah. God promised that as long as Solomon remained obedient, his kingdom would stand firm and would not be divided.
God's promises to you, as a child of God, are as reliable as His promises to David and Solomon. You can trust God… to be God!

Thursday • 1 Chronicles 28:20-29:9

Q&A

DIGGING DEEPER • We have heard the phrase "Put your money where your mouth is," which means that it is better to do something than just talk about it. If we say we love the Lord, then our actions and attitudes should be evidence of that. In today's passage the people of Israel put their money where their mouth was and gave toward the construction of the temple. David modeled his love for the Lord by gathering mounds of silver, gold, and wood for the building of the temple. David asked the people to display their love for the Lord by giving from their resources. When we love the Lord we will give him our obedience, time, and money. God doesn't ask for all of our cash, but our willingness to give shows our love for Him.
Talk to your pastor or leader about giving tithes and offerings to God. Then read Malachi 3:10-11 about giving to the Lord.

Friday • 1 Chronicles 29:10-19

DIGGING DEEPER • David addresses the greatness of God and that everything belongs to Him. He speaks of some of God's attributes and characteristics, among them eternality (forever and ever), omnipotence (all-powerful), and sovereignty ("all… in heaven and earth is thine…exalted as head above all"). He notes that God is man's provider, and moves on to offer praise and thanksgiving, confessing that even the gifts that he and the people had given toward the temple had come from God. His question, "But who am I, and what is my people that they should be able to offer so willingly after this sort?" indicated that David knew Israel's history. God had taken David from the sheepfold to the palace. Only God could do that.
Ask your parents or other adults in your church about their salvation experiences. Compare their situations before they were saved and now.

Saturday • 1 Chronicles 29:20-30

DIGGING DEEPER • When we see a building being built in town or a house going up in our neighborhood, we understand that someone provided the money for those builders to do the work. Today, David and the people give praise and worship to the Lord they loved for all He had provided and for His power and sovereignty. They worshiped by prostrating themselves: falling on their knees with their foreheads to the ground. On the next day, they followed up on their prayers of dedication with sacrifices of communion with God and one another, and by offering burnt offerings. Some 3,000 animals were offered, and their giving brought them great gladness before the Lord.
When you worship the Lord in church, in your Word of Life Club, or at home, make a list of what He has done for you and praise Him for it.

qt WEEK 33

Think of a time when you had to write a term paper or study for a major test. Remember how great it was to have it done, and how you felt like celebrating? This week we will see an incredible time of worship and celebration as Solomon and the people of Israel celebrate the completion of the Lord's temple.

Prayer focus for this week

Q: The Question — *What is the writer saying?*
A: The Answer — *How Can I apply this to my life?*

Sunday • 2 Chronicles 1:1-12

DIGGING DEEPER • What if a genie suddenly appeared and offered you a wish? Would you wish for riches, fame, or power? Well, we know there is no such thing as a magic genie, but in today's passage, God appears before Solomon and tells him to ask for anything he wants. Notice that God appears only after Solomon had worshipped Him, and that Solomon's response was to praise God and acknowledge what He had already done. Solomon unselfishly asked God to grant him wisdom and knowledge so that he could lead his people. Solomon was more concerned with God's purpose than with the temporary things of this world. God recognized this and gave Solomon more than he could have imagined.
Do you approach God with humility, or do you simply ask Him to grant your selfish wants and desires? Pray that God would give you spiritual wisdom.

Monday • 2 Chronicles 5:1-14

Q
A

DIGGING DEEPER • Have you ever been part of a surprise party? So much work goes into getting all of the guests, decorations, and food in place, but, even then, the celebration is incomplete until the guest of honor arrives. King Solomon has been overseeing the construction of the temple for over thirteen years, and now it is time to celebrate as the guest of honor (God) is officially invited into the temple. Solomon and the priests knew that the Ark represented the presence of God, so they took great care in transporting the Ark and bringing it into the temple. God showed His approval of the temple by filling it with His holy presence. **Do you treat your church as a holy place? The church is found in the body of Christ and not in a building, but we should always treat God's house with the reverence it deserves.**

Tuesday • 2 Chronicles 6:1-11

Q
A

DIGGING DEEPER • When the temple was completed, Solomon recognized that it was a fulfillment of a promise that God had made to his father (See 2 Samuel 7:14-17). David had a desire to build a temple for the Lord, but because of his sin, God told David that it would be his son who would actually build it. Even though Solomon had overseen this incredible construction project, he understood that it was God who had done it, and was quick to give all the praise to Him. This story reminds us that God is faithful to forgive our sin, but that sin brings consequences that include missing out on God's blessings for our lives. **Think of a time when you have seen God's faithfulness in a particular situation. Did you recognize His faithfulness and praise Him for it? Is there a sin that might be robbing you of God's blessing for your life?**

Wednesday • 2 Chronicles 6:12-21

Q&A

DIGGING DEEPER • How far would you travel and how long would you stand in line for a chance to meet the president, a famous athlete, or an actor? You would likely be stressed about how you looked and what you were going to say. Isn't it interesting that as believers we have unlimited access to the Creator of the universe, and yet many of us rarely make the effort to talk to Him? In Solomon's prayer, he wonders how the same God whom even the highest heavens cannot contain could possibly dwell in the temple he had built. God chose to make His presence available in the temple, and He chooses to make Himself available in our lives.
Do you take for granted the relationship with God that is available to you through Jesus Christ? Is it possible that the reason you never talk to Him is because no true relationship exists?

Thursday • 2 Chronicles 6:22-31

Q&A

DIGGING DEEPER • 2, 4, 6, 8, 10… Do you see a pattern developing with these numbers? As Solomon prays for his people, we see a pattern develop in these hypothetical situations. In each of these examples, God's judgment comes only after His people have sinned against Him. God's forgiveness comes only after His people have confessed and repented of their sin. Because of Christ's work on the cross, the sins of believers have already been forgiven. God still desires us to confess and turn from our sin on a daily basis. God understands that unconfessed sin leads to broken fellowship with Him.
God does not take sin lightly, but He is quick to forgive us when we confess our sin and repent of it. Are you willing not only to admit your wrongdoing, but to turn away from it and turn back to Him?

Friday • 2 Chronicles 6:32-42

Q&A

DIGGING DEEPER • As Solomon concludes his prayer of dedication for the temple, he turns his attention beyond his own people and nation. Solomon now asks the Lord to hear and answer the prayers of any foreigners who might come to the temple, so that they might also know and fear the Lord. In this prayer, Solomon shows a desire to see all people know the Lord. Solomon's prayer provides us with a great example of how believers should pray. Just like Solomon, we should pray for the protection and faithfulness of our fellow Christians. We should also pray that the lost of this world would come to know Jesus Christ as Savior.
Is your prayer life one that is exclusively focused on yourself, or do you regularly lift up the people around you? Pray today that God would strengthen you and other believers to reach a lost world for Christ.

Saturday • 2 Chronicles 7:1-11

Q&A

DIGGING DEEPER • Think back to the best party or celebration you personally experienced. Was it a wedding, birthday, New Year's party, or state title for your school? Now imagine a celebration that lasts for over two weeks. The Lord showed His approval by filling the temple and accepting the offerings and sacrifices of the people. They continued to celebrate with sacrifices, worship, and music for fourteen more days, until Solomon finally sent them home with joy in their hearts. Notice the people's joy was due to the great things God had done. David and Solomon had only been vessels for God's great plan.
God's approval comes any time we complete a task that He has asked of us. Seek today to be faithful in the little things that God has for you, and realize that our faithfulness is always something to celebrate.

WEEK 34

The old expression says that "change is inevitable." That will certainly be true in this week's passages. We will go from the height of Solomon's kingdom to a son who wasn't ready to rule, and then to a king who had no choice but to trust the Lord. In all of this, we will see everything change except the faithfulness of God.

Prayer focus for this week

Q: The Question — *What is the writer saying?*
A: The Answer — *How Can I apply this to my life?*

Sunday • 2 Chronicles 7:12-22

DIGGING DEEPER • Today's passage is God's response to Solomon's prayer in chapter 6. God explains that in order for His blessings to be received, there must be humility, prayer, devotion to Him, and repentance of sin. The rest of this passage includes both a promise and a warning to Solomon. The promise was that as long as he followed and obeyed God, his family line would continue to rule over Israel. The warning was that if Solomon and Israel turned away and served other gods, then God would uproot both Israel and the temple. Later, Solomon does worship other gods, and history shows he was judged by God. He keeps His Word! **Do you take seriously the warnings that God has given us in the Bible concerning evil and sin, or do you play around with these things? 1 Corinthians 6:18 tells us to flee immorality. Heed that advice today.**

Monday • 2 Chronicles 9:1-14

DIGGING DEEPER • Have you ever heard the expression "You have to see it to believe it" used to describe something amazing? Queen Sheba had heard about the achievements and wisdom of King Solomon, but evidently thought that it all sounded too good to be true. Once she had talked with him, Sheba was convinced that Solomon's wisdom exceeded the reports that she had heard. She lavished him with gifts and even praised Solomon's God (although there is no evidence that she accepted Him as her own). Notice when Sheba gave Solomon such generous gifts, he immediately used them to honor and worship the Lord.
Do you use the things God has given you (abilities, time, possessions, etc.) to honor, glorify, and worship Him? Is the spiritual blessing of your salvation obvious to those around you?

Tuesday • 2 Chronicles 9:15-31

DIGGING DEEPER • It would be easy to miss the lesson found in today's passage. Here we see a description of Solomon's glory and wealth. God came to Solomon at the beginning of his reign and told him to ask for whatever he wanted. Solomon asked for wisdom and knowledge so he could lead the people of Israel. Yesterday we saw how Solomon had been blessed with great wisdom, but today we see that God had blessed him with so much more. God's desire is to give us more than we could ever ask for or imagine, but we must first display a pure heart and a desire to see only God's name glorified.
Do you recognize all the blessings that God has given you? Are the things you ask of Him motivated by a desire to see Him honored or by a craving for worldly things?

Wednesday • 2 Chronicles 12:5-16

Q/A

DIGGING DEEPER • How quickly things can change! It's only been five years since the reign of Solomon, but things are very different. Solomon's son, Rehoboam, is now king, and he and Israel have abandoned the law of the Lord. God allows them to be attacked and the temple and palace treasures to be taken. By not focusing on God, Rehoboam allowed the Israelites to turn away from the Lord. The failures of Rehoboam are summarized in verse 14: "And he did evil, because he prepared not his heart to seek the LORD." He had witnessed his father faithfully serve God, but he had failed to develop his own relationship with the Lord. **Even the blessing of growing up in a Christian home is no guarantee of your own spiritual growth. We must prepare our hearts and seek the Lord on a daily basis. Failure to do so will ultimately lead us into evil.**

Thursday • 2 Chronicles 15:1-15

Q/A

DIGGING DEEPER • Wet Paint…Danger Ahead…Beware of Dog! Sometimes the simplest warnings are the most effective. Today we see God deliver a simple but powerful warning. God simply reminds Asa that as long as he seeks the Lord, he will find Him, but if he abandons God, then God will abandon him. As simple as this warning might seem, it unfortunately was one that Israel had forgotten on a number of occasions. Asa took the words of the Lord to heart and removed the idols out of the land and restored the temple. Asa's leadership led his people to take an oath to seek the LORD…with all their heart…and soul.
Do you recognize that God is a jealous God who wants all your heart and life? Is there a sin that may be affecting your relationship with Him? Learn from Israel's failures and seek Him today.

Friday • 2 Chronicles 20:1-13

DIGGING DEEPER • They're coming! A massive army is coming, and they're not far away! This was the message that Jehoshaphat received in chapter 20. Jehoshaphat is now king and is faced with an unexpected attack on his kingdom. Although alarmed, he immediately calls on the kingdom to fast while he seeks the Lord. Even though Jehoshaphat didn't know what to do (v. 12), he was wise enough to know that he needed God. Jehoshaphat's prayer simply asked God to judge this army because Judah did not have the power to fight them. Jehoshaphat realized that sometimes in life, prayer is the only hope and God is the only answer. **Is there a problem or circumstance that you just don't know how to handle? Surrender it to the Lord today, and ask Him to take control.**

Saturday • 2 Chronicles 20:14-30

DIGGING DEEPER • Yesterday, Jehoshaphat asked God to judge the attacking army because Judah was powerless to fight. Today, God comforts Judah and tells them not to fear because, "…the battle is not yours, but God's." God then tells them to stand still and see how miraculously the Lord delivers them. God literally allowed the people of Judah to stand and sing while He defeated their enemies. Not only did He completely destroy the enemy's army, but the treasure left behind was more than the Israelites could collect. This is a great lesson for us today. When we place our faith and trust in God, He can deliver us from our enemies. **Do you give God the opportunity to work in the circumstances of your life, or are you too busy running around trying to fix things yourself? Remind yourself today that the battle is not yours, but God's.**

qt WEEK 35

"Here to there, and back again" might be the best way to describe this week's study. We see a kingdom that has completely turned away from God, a son that leads it back into God's favor, and, finally, a wicked king whose stubborn pride ultimately leaves Judah in ruins.

Prayer focus for this week

Q: The Question — *What is the writer saying?*
A: The Answer — *How Can I apply this to my life?*

Sunday • 2 Chronicles 29:1-11

DIGGING DEEPER • As we move from Chapter 20 to 29, over 100 years have passed and seven different kings have ruled. Hezekiah took over the throne from his wicked father, Ahaz, who had closed the doors of the temple (28:24) and encouraged idol worship. Verse 2 tells us that Hezekiah did that which was right in the sight of the LORD. Even though he walked into a bad situation, Hezekiah was not content to let it stay that way. He immediately reopened the temple and began the process of purifying and repairing it. Hezekiah was committed to God and to leaving things better than he had found them.

Do you feel like the spiritual condition of your family, friends, or school is so bad that it is hopeless? Nothing is hopeless with God. You may not be able to do everything, but you can do something. Get started today!

Monday • 2 Chronicles 29:27-36

Q
A

DIGGING DEEPER • 2,592,000 seconds, 43,200 minutes, 720 hours, or 30 days. All of these represent the amount of time in a month. In less than a month, God had used Hezekiah to reopen the temple, cleanse and repair it, and restore temple worship. Hezekiah's sincere desire to lead Judah back to the Lord had turned God's anger away from them. God helped them restore worship in the temple, and the people responded with a variety of offerings and sacrifices. Hezekiah and the people were amazed because God was able to do all of this so quickly. Once again, God had shown that He was ever faithful.
Our God is not limited by time, resources, or impossible circumstances. With Him all things are possible. Give Him complete control of your life, and see what He can do.

Tuesday • 2 Chronicles 30:1-12

Q
A

DIGGING DEEPER • After restoring the temple, Hezekiah's next order of business was to reinstate the Passover celebration that his father had neglected. Hezekiah sent out a strong message encouraging the people to return to the Lord so that they might be spared God's fierce anger. Hezekiah pled with the people to "be ye not stiff-necked (stubborn), as your fathers were, but yield yourselves unto the LORD." Notice that some responded to Hezekiah's request with mockery, while others repented and returned to Jerusalem. When God calls us to repent, it will always generate a response of either humility or a hardened heart.
Can you think of a time when God has convicted you of a particular sin in your life? Was your response one of humility and repentance, or of pride and stubbornness?

Wednesday • 2 Chronicles 30:18-27

DIGGING DEEPER • Have you ever heard the expression "It's what's on the inside that counts"? Hezekiah's plea drew a large crowd to Jerusalem for the Passover celebration. Many of the people who came had not been purified as the Law required (Exodus 12), but still took part in the Passover meal. Even though this went against the Law, God chose to heal the people. God is always more concerned with what's going on inside our hearts than He is with our outward actions. Jesus echoed this idea in His dealings with the Pharisees (Matthew 15). God's grace is not about what we do, but about what Christ has done.
Are you more concerned with looking like a Christian than with actually being one? Even if we fool everyone around us, we don't fool Him. Ask God to help you be an authentic follower of Christ.

Thursday • 2 Chronicles 33:1-10

DIGGING DEEPER • "If you can't say something nice, don't say anything at all." If we followed this motto concerning Hezekiah's son, Manasseh, then today's page might be blank. Even though he had seen his father faithfully serve the Lord, Manasseh was a wicked king that "did that which was evil in the sight of the LORD." Manasseh restored idol worship, brought idols into the very temple that God had inhabited, practiced sorcery and witchcraft, and even killed his sons for human sacrifice. Ultimately verse 9 tells us that he led his nation away from God and into evil. Manasseh's life is a tragic example of a life lived apart from God
Verse 10 tells us that the Lord spoke to Manasseh, but he did not listen. Is God trying to get your attention about a sin in your life, but you're ignoring Him? Learn from Manasseh's mistake before it's too late.

Friday • 2 Chronicles 33:11-19

DIGGING DEEPER • "He got what he deserved." This is how we might react to Manasseh's fate in today's passage. Taken prisoner and bound in shackles, Manasseh's situation seemed hopeless. In a moment of desperation, Manasseh humbled himself and called out to God. The Lord was moved by his plea, brought him out of bondage, and back to Jerusalem. Verse 13 tells us that Manasseh knew from this that the Lord was God, and sought to undo all the wrong he had done. Even though God forgave Manasseh, his sin had consequences and began Judah's downward spiral into exile.

God never wants us to get what we deserve. The greatest example of this is Jesus Christ. We deserve death and hell, but Christ's work on the cross gives each of us the opportunity to enjoy forgiveness and heaven.

Saturday • 2 Chronicles 36:11-21

DIGGING DEEPER • Today we see a stark contrast between King Zedekiah and King Manasseh from yesterday's passage. Scripture tells us that both of them did that which was evil in the sight of the LORD (33:2, 36:12), but there was a big difference between them. Manasseh had turned away from God, but in desperation called upon Him for deliverance. Zedekiah's pride led to continued resistance and a hardened heart. Zedekiah's people were no better, and actually mocked the words of the messengers that God sent to warn them. God ultimately judged them through Nebuchadnezzar, who destroyed Jerusalem and took Judah into exile.

Is God once again speaking to you through this passage? God will try again and again to get your attention, but He will not be mocked. Don't allow pride to keep you away from Him. Call upon the Lord today.

WEEK 36

As you look into the Scripture this week, Peter will give some basic instructions for living the Christian life. He will remind you of your future and what God did for you. He will give you some practical advice for living godly. When this week is finished, you should be excited about being on God's team. Read on!

Prayer focus for this week

Q: The Question — *What is the writer saying?*
A: The Answer — *How Can I apply this to my life?*

Sunday • 1 Peter 1:1-8

DIGGING DEEPER • As you walk into the room, you see the perfect place to sit. How in the world did everyone else miss it? As you get closer, you see the sign: Reserved. Reserved... what a frustrating word that can be, unless of course, it is reserved for you. As Peter begins his letter to believers scattered throughout the region, he reminds them that because they are saved, they have a place set aside for them in Heaven. What a joy to know that all Christians are kept by the power of God (v. 5)! Despite what trials (v. 6) the world may send our way and despite the fact that we have never seen Jesus (v. 8), we can be joyful because our future is secure. We have a place reserved for us.

Will you stop right now and thank God for the fact that He makes your future secure? Who needs you to explain to him the way to a secure future?

Monday • 1 Peter 1:9-16

DIGGING DEEPER • So, you are saved! You asked Jesus to be your Savior and you are not going to hell. And that's it! Sadly, that is it for a lot of immature Christians. "Don't ask me to live like a Christian," they say with their lifestyle, "that ain't cool." The Apostle Peter; however, makes some pretty bold statements. He says, "Not fashioning (conforming) yourselves according to your former lusts (evil desires)." In other words, the way you handle yourself should not be like the world. In contrast, you should live holy–totally separate from sin and evil. The way you dress should be holy. The way you talk should be holy. The way you look should be holy. The things you listen to or look at should be holy. "Be ye holy in all manner of conversation [lifestyle] ...Be ye holy, for I am holy."
What part of your lifestyle looks like the world? What needs to change?

Tuesday • 1 Peter 1:17-25

DIGGING DEEPER • What is the most expensive gift you have ever received? How did you respond when you got it? It feels great to know that someone thought enough about you to get you a gift of such value. The Apostle Peter reminds us of a priceless gift that was given for us. God had a plan, even before the world began (v. 20), for Jesus to die for us. It was a gift more expensive than gold or silver (v. 18). God thought about us! If we have accepted His great gift of love, we should love the brethren (v. 22). As if the gift was not enough, Peter reminds us that the gift is secure. We received this gift through the incorruptible Word of God. What a thought! We have received from God a priceless, eternal gift that He decided to give us before we even existed.
When did you last thank God for thinking about you in such a profound way? With whom will you share your gift?

Wednesday • 1 Peter 2:1-10

Q&A

DIGGING DEEPER • Can you remember what it was like when you first joined a sports team or when you got that new job? You might not have known exactly how to act or what to do. Hopefully at some point a coach, a boss, a teammate, or a co-worker made you feel like you were truly part of the team. Peter reminds us of the team we have joined. He reminds us of Jesus, the Chief Cornerstone (v. 6). He reminds us that we are part of the body of Christ (v. 5). He reminds us that we have been chosen and called out of darkness (v. 9) and we have obtained God's mercy (v. 10). He also reminds us that our Cornerstone is offensive to some (vv. 7-8). Being a Christian is so much more than the individual Christian, since we are part of something greater than ourselves.

How can you be more of a team player this week? How would you show forth the praises of Him?

Thursday • 1 Peter 2:11-17

Q&A

DIGGING DEEPER • "I thought you were a Christian." What sad words to have to hear. The Apostle Peter strongly encourages each Christian to live in the world but separate from the world. The world loves to speak out against God's people. When a Christian openly sins, it gives the unsaved world ammunition to take a shot at the name of Christ. Peter urges us to be submissive to the rules of men and to place ourselves under the appropriate authorities. By doing so, we can shut the mouths of any would-be mud-slingers. Remember, this world is not our permanent home. We are but "strangers and pilgrims" (v. 11).

What can you do to improve your Christian reputation with the unsaved world? What steps can you take to protect your name, the name of your church, and the precious name of Jesus from those who would defame them?

Friday • 1 Peter 2:18-25

DIGGING DEEPER • Occasionally in sports, a player will take a cheap shot at another player. He might make a late hit. He might slide tackle away from the play, or he might slide into second spikes high. But do you know who usually gets into trouble? Not the cheap shot guy, but the guy who retaliates. Peter reminds us of how we are to act when we get the short end of the stick. He tells us that God is pleased when we receive persecution patiently. Our example is Jesus Christ Himself. He deserved nothing that He endured on the cross. Yet as He hung there, His only words about those who were killing Him were words of forgiveness. He endured death on the cross. He is our example. Follow His steps.
In what area of life are you experiencing suffering? How can you be like Christ in that area? Will you follow the suffering steps of Jesus?

Saturday • 1 Peter 3:1-7

DIGGING DEEPER • So, you're not a wife and you're not a husband; therefore, this passage doesn't apply to you, right? Wrong! Oh, you may not be married right now, but one day you might be, and these lessons are so much easier to learn now than they will be later. Ladies, decide right now that when you are married you will live in subjection to your husband. Begin adorning yourself, not with a bunch of clothes that draw attention to your body, but by putting on a meek and quiet spirit. Guys, determine right now that forsaking all others, you will love the girl you will one day marry. Love her so much that, even now, you will keep yourself pure for only her. Gals, commit to keeping yourself pure for your future husband.
What can you do right now that will improve your future marriage? How can you prepare yourself for your future spouse?

qt WEEK 37

The Christian life is not all fun and games. Unfortunately, the Christian life can be difficult and filled with suffering. This week, Peter will give you some practical advice on how to deal with undeserved suffering. He will discuss the hard work that it takes to live godly. Hang on for some help with the difficult times in life.

Prayer focus for this week

Q: The Question — *What is the writer saying?*
A: The Answer — *How Can I apply this to my life?*

Sunday • 1 Peter 3:8-12

DIGGING DEEPER • Have you ever wondered what it would take to have a good life? Maybe if you had brand name clothes, a fancy foreign car, stacks of cash, and the face of a movie star, you would have a good life. If you watch television or go to the movies, those things seem to be the secret. Well, here is the real secret. If you want to "love life and see good days" (v. 10), you must speak no evil (v. 10), see no evil (v. 11), and seek peace (v.11). Since God is watching the righteous and listening to their prayers, we should live in unity with love and courtesy. When someone does us wrong, we should not return the wrongdoing, but give him the mercy of a blessing. What is your life like? Are you trying to find the good life from the world? **From what evil do you need to run? What steps do you need to take to be more unified with your fellow Christians?**

Monday • 1 Peter 3:13-22

DIGGING DEEPER • Today's topic: More suffering. "Oh, great," you say, "that's really encouraging." Actually, it can be encouraging. We know that we are going to suffer, but "who is he that will harm you [us], if ye [we] be followers of that which is good?" Peter reminds us that, in the midst of the suffering, we should have already decided that God will be our priority and we will use that suffering as an opportunity to share our faith. Jesus, who did not deserve to die, suffered and died for us. He is our example. If the ungodly world tries to accuse us of evil, our lifestyle should be so holy that no one would ever believe the lie (v. 16).
Does your lifestyle cause others to ask about Jesus? If the world made accusations against your Christian character, would others believe them? What can you do this week to strengthen your character?

Tuesday • 1 Peter 4:1-6

DIGGING DEEPER • If someone in your school hosted a party involving an illegal activity, would you get invited? The question is not "Would you go?" but "Would you get invited?" Do you have a reputation that excludes you from such invitations? Do you live in such a way that others know not to even give you an invitation because you would never entertain the thought of attending? Peter, speaking of fellow believers, reports that the world thinks it is strange that these believers do not act the way they used to (vv. 3-4). As a result, they received undeserved scorn. Remember, we will ultimately be judged by Jesus Christ. Live today in such a way as to please Him, not the in crowd.
Do you fit in with ungodly people? How have you changed since accepting Jesus Christ as your Savior? How will you improve your reputation as a Christian?

Wednesday • 1 Peter 4:7-11

Q&A

DIGGING DEEPER • How much do you love others? Peter very clearly says, "...above all things have fervent charity [love] among yourselves" (v. 8). Since we are to have love "above all," how should we go about loving others? Well, verse 9 tells us to be hospitable and not hold grudges. Verse 10 tells us to use the gift, talent or ability that we have to minister to others. So, naturally, we can show our love to others in these three ways: be hospitable, do not hold grudges, and minister with our abilities. If you do not have a venue to use your spiritual gift, contact your pastor or youth pastor for some suggestions. As we love in these ways, God is glorified (v. 11).
To whom can you be hospitable this week? How will you do it? What gifts have you been given? How will you use them this week?

Thursday • 1 Peter 4:12-19

Q&A

DIGGING DEEPER • Have you ever watched a news report that showed someone being arrested? Many times the suspect will hide his face in shame. His unlawful actions are the cause for coming problems. His future suffering is well deserved. But what about those who suffer because they are Christians? Peter encourages them to hold their heads up high because their suffering in Christ shows that the Spirit of God is upon them (v. 14). Peter warns us, however, to live righteously so we do not receive deserved suffering. He also reminds us that when God judges, He begins with His own children (v. 17).
How can you give God glory through your suffering? If God were to judge you today, what would be the outcome? What can you work on this week that would help you be prepared for coming judgment?

Friday • 1 Peter 5:1-7

DIGGING DEEPER • How do you feel when someone tells you to do something that they refuse to do themselves? It is kind of frustrating, isn't it? Peter gave the elders of the church a few basic instructions. He told them to take charge of the children of God (v. 2). They were not supposed to be dictators, but examples of how to live. We are to follow the example of the elders and be humble. In doing so, God will exalt us when the time is right (v. 6). How much easier it is to be humble when our elders are humble! Even Peter shows his willingness to follow his own teaching. In verse 1, while speaking of himself, he says, "…who am also an elder." Peter lived what he preached. Because he is a great example, we can find it easier to obey. **Do you practice what you preach? What kind of example are you being to those younger than you? How can you improve this week?**

Saturday • 1 Peter 5:8-14

DIGGING DEEPER • Have you ever seen someone pretend to be a basketball superstar? As he shoots the ball, he can be heard saying, "Three, two, one, it's over! We win!" Why don't you ever see someone in push-up position, acting like a hero? "Ninety-eight, ninety-nine, one hundred…and the crowd goes wild!" The truth is the months of training, the dedication to the game, and the hard work are the reasons for the glory. The last-second shot can happen because the work has happened. The athlete must suffer before he will receive glory. Peter reminds us that we are called to glory (v. 10), but we must first endure suffering. The suffering will mature, establish, strengthen, and settle us (v. 10). When that happens, God can be glorified in our lives. **What is your attitude toward suffering? Begin today to grow and bring glory to God?**

qt WEEK 38

Ever wonder if God is really doing something in your life? Are we just floating through life? That's how a whole nation felt, and one guy in particular. Is God active? You bet He is, and wait until you see how much! The Lord is always at work! The question is... "Am I ready for God to be radically active in my life?"

Prayer focus for this week

Q: The Question — *What is the writer saying?*
A: The Answer — *How can I apply this to my life?*

Sunday • Exodus 1:1-14

DIGGING DEEPER • Exodus follows the Book of Genesis, so that's where we will start. What we first notice is Egypt's attitude toward Israel. We learn the real reason Israel is oppressed and persecuted, and it's fear. Verses 8-11 lay it out very clearly. Ever been bullied? Someone is just being mean for no apparent reason. It's often because of fear – not on our part, but on the bully's. He's afraid of being rejected or hated. That might sound strange, because people would actually like him better if he weren't a bully. Fear rarely makes sense. Love is just the opposite – it cares instead of persecutes. It reaches out instead of lashes out. Either way, we often grow when we are persecuted; however, it rarely benefits the bully.
How do you treat others of whom you are afraid? How can you show love to someone who dislikes you?

Monday • Exodus 1:15-22

Q
A

DIGGING DEEPER • You've got a choice – a party or a Bible study. If you go to the Bible study, you'll make your Christian friends happy, but disappoint your other friends. If you go to the party, you'll make the popular people happy, and maybe they'll like you more, but your Christian friends won't be too impressed. A no-win situation, huh? The question is, whom do you want to please – others or God? Our decisions don't often threaten our lives, but that was the case for these midwives. They chose to please God. They probably assumed they were dead for disobeying a tyrant Pharaoh. Nonetheless, God protected them and blessed them with families of their own. Take a step of faith, even if it doesn't look good for you today.
Are you more concerned about what others think or what God thinks? What friend do you need to be careful about following, rather than God?

Tuesday • Exodus 2:1-10

Q
A

DIGGING DEEPER • It's amazing what God can do! By faith, Moses' mother put Moses in a basket and hid him in the tall weeds (Hebrews 11:23). Sounds crazy, doesn't it, to put a three-month-old baby in a basket and place it in the river? Moses' mother trusted the Lord to take care of him. She gave into God's care what was most precious to her. I can almost hear Moses' mother pray, "Somehow, someway – take care of him." And that's exactly what the Lord did. In fact, the baby came back to his mother, and she was able to nurse him and take care of him…and get paid for it! She even had the protection of Pharaoh – the very person who was trying to kill all the baby boys! Faith is blind to the impossible.
In what situation does it seem impossible for you to trust the Lord? Are you willing to give to God the most important thing you have, for His glory?

Wednesday • Exodus 2:11-25

DIGGING DEEPER • Things get pretty dicey for Moses today! Moses had a pretty cushy life growing up in Pharaoh's home, but he still felt bad for his people. Is it ever right to do wrong in order to bring about something good? Never! It was wrong for Moses to kill the Egyptian. Moses' desire to see his people treated fairly or rescued from the Egyptians was good, but there was a different way to go about it. That's hard! Moses is going to start learning about faith. He didn't trust the Lord, so he took matters into his own hands. God's ways are always best, even when things don't seem fair. The question is whether we have the courage to continue to live for God and trust Him to take care of the details.
Have you asked the Lord to forgive you for taking matters into your own hands? Would you pray and put the difficult situation into His hands?

Thursday • Exodus 3:1-12

DIGGING DEEPER • The Lord comes to Moses in a powerful way. God could have spoken to him any way He wanted. Why did He use a burning bush that didn't burn up? Here's why: it's impossible for a bush to be on fire, and not burn up. It cannot happen except when God is involved! The Lord knew Moses' response before He told him to go back to Egypt. It was probably something like, "I can't do that – it's impossible." The difference is what the Lord told him in the beginning of verse 12. Not only did Moses have to face his fear, but he also had to do something he never thought he could. Are you ready for God to challenge you like this?
Are you willing to step out and believe that the Lord will give you strength far beyond yourself? What is impossible for you right now? Would you pray and commit it to the Lord?

Friday • Exodus 3:13-22

DIGGING DEEPER • Moses starts questioning God – big-time. We all probably would. But God's first answer should have been enough for Moses. God calls himself "I AM." That's a strange name, but this is what God told Moses: I exist. I am established. Not I am…something, like big or awesome. Just…I AM. Almost like, I AM everything, or I can do anything. The point is that whatever objection we have. GOD IS the answer. Always. What about Pharaoh? I AM…God, and he's just a man. What about Egypt's army? I AM…stronger than any army. There is no challenge or difficulty that God's I AM cannot overcome!
Today, fill in the blank for whatever you face. God is your "I AM ____." Do you live like you are your own "I AM"? I can handle it, or I can do it? What is it that you need to trust God for today? Will you do it?

Saturday • Exodus 4:1-17

DIGGING DEEPER • Why would God ever use me? That was Moses' objection. The amazing thing about this whole passage is that God delights in using people just like us. We usually think of Moses as this great leader, one of the godliest men of the Old Testament, but not here. Moses sounds like a wimp. But that's the amazing thing: God wants to use ordinary people like us! Even a stick and some water from the river can become great instruments with God's power. You already have something great right now that God can use for His glory. So what is it – your singing ability, popularity, money, friendliness, compassion, athletics, smarts, a car, an extra pen or pencil, or maybe a tract? God can use anything or anyone!
Think through the list above or come up with your own things that God can use. Then ask the Lord to use whatever you have to honor and glorify Him.

qt WEEK 39

This week is awesome! How do you go from feeling spiritual to being spiritual? That's what we see in Moses this week. Notice that it all happens while Moses is serving God. He's very busy doing what the Lord wants. That kind of change doesn't happen while you are on the sidelines in the Christian game of life.

Prayer focus for this week

Q: The Question — *What is the writer saying?*
A: The Answer — *How Can I apply this to my life?*

Sunday • Exodus 4:18-31

DIGGING DEEPER • Ever feel like a 100-pound weakling trying to guard a 300-pound football player? This is a mismatch! Moses might have felt like that. The Lord reminds Moses to perform the miracles that He had instructed and empowered him to do. He was fully equipped. So why did the Lord want to kill Moses? Perhaps because he was still not fully trusting the Lord and willing to obey Him in all things. Circumcision was important to God, and Moses had neglected to take care of that matter with his son. When it was resolved, he was able to move on and do whatever the Lord asked of him. As he performed the miracles, the people of Israel believed God, just as God said they would. Now there are bigger opportunities awaiting him. **Are you confident the Lord will strengthen you to do what He desires? Even though Moses was afraid, he still obeyed. What will you do?**

Monday • Exodus 5:1-12

DIGGING DEEPER • Here's an easy question: is life always easy, even when you do the right thing? Duh! Sometimes things may get difficult, even when we obey the Lord. Most of us don't want life to be difficult, but the question is whether or not we're obeying God. The Lord does bless us for obedience. The really difficult times only last for a season. Here's the amazing thing: when the hard times pass, we usually think, "I'd rather have gone through the hard time and obeyed God, than just have had an easy life." Can you picture yourself saying that? Many believers have found that to be true, because the Lord blesses and brings His children through safely.
Are you shying away from something difficult that the Lord wants you to do? Do you trust yourself rather than God?

Tuesday • Exodus 5:13-23

DIGGING DEEPER • Wow! Things are really getting tough for Moses. It's not just Pharaoh who's unhappy now. It's Moses' own people! Maybe you're saying, "OK, this has gone too far, I wouldn't stick with what Moses is doing." But Moses does the right thing. He simply asks God, Why? He's not accusing God of doing wrong. He just doesn't understand. We don't always get the answer we want today, but not everything is in our timing. If Moses could have seen the whole Book of Exodus, it would have been much easier for him to obey, but then he never would have had to trust God each day. He learned this lesson earlier when he killed the Egyptian. Trust God's timing, even when it doesn't make sense or seem fair.
Are you patient enough to let God work in His timing? What situation do you face today? What are you going to do when it gets difficult?

Wednesday • Exodus 6:1-13

DIGGING DEEPER • Moses has a big problem. He probably feels like he is in way over his head. Have you ever felt that way when it comes to obeying the Lord? Go back to the passage and check this out. How many times does the Lord say "I will"? The Lord does not talk about what Moses has to do, but what God is already going to do (vv. 6-8). The Lord had a perfect plan for Moses, and it was to bring the people out of Egypt. At this point, Moses needs to believe God, obey Him, and watch the Lord do it. God's Word is full of promises for us to claim, just as Moses did. Verses 10-12 show Moses giving the Lord another objection. But the truth is, the Lord does the work. He's just waiting for us to follow Him.
In what is God waiting for you to follow Him? Do you feel pressure to do what God already said He will do? Will you trust Him to do the work?

Thursday • Exodus 6:28-7:13

DIGGING DEEPER • Today starts the first of many times that Moses and Aaron come before Pharaoh, confronting him with God's plan. Sometimes facing our friends or boss can be just as challenging as facing Pharaoh. Keep in mind yesterday's passage, and all the times God said, "I will." The neat thing in today's passage is that Moses and Aaron do just as the Lord commanded them. Even though Pharaoh's magicians fake a miracle, the Lord shows them that He is still greater by having Aaron's snake eat the others. I'm sure Moses and Aaron were surprised to see the other snakes. Perhaps they thought, "This wasn't part of the plan!" That probably made them nervous, but the Lord proved to Moses that He was with them!
Are you willing to trust God while you are serving Him, even when things don't go just as you expect? Are you avoiding an opportunity to serve?

Friday • Exodus 7:14-25

Q
A

DIGGING DEEPER • "Two plus two does not equal four! I refuse to believe it, and I'm going to ignore everyone else, and show the whole world I'm right and they're wrong!" Not very smart, huh? Today we see another cheap trick to imitate God's awesome power. That's what Pharaoh's magicians did. When someone doesn't want to believe God, they'll go to any length to ignore Him. Verses 22-23 show Pharaoh's attitude about this. Unfortunately, ignoring God and His truth doesn't just affect you. It hurts others as well, such as brothers, sisters, parents, and friends, even those to whom you should be witnessing. Now, all of Egypt has no water!
Am I being stubborn toward God? Who gets hurt around me when I don't obey God? Whom can I ask to help me not to ignore God in my daily life?

Saturday • Exodus 8:1-15

Q
A

DIGGING DEEPER • Frogs, Frogs, Frogs! They even went up on the people. The magicians produced more frogs, and it only made the problem worse. "That's a good idea! Yeah, I didn't think we had enough frogs around here. I'm glad the magicians made more!" The real test would have been if they had made the frogs go away! It's interesting that Pharaoh asked Moses to pray for help for them. Moses let Pharaoh pick the time to give them relief, to prove that it was no trick. It was as if Moses forced Pharaoh to prove that God was God, the only "I AM." Why would Pharaoh keep this up and not give in? He wanted to keep Israel as his slaves. But there's more to it as we keep going in the story. It only gets worse!
Do you ever pray and ask God for help while not obeying him? What sin should you ask God to forgive before you ask for other things?

qt WEEK 40

Plague after plague this week. That might sound boring, but each one has its own unique part. It's not just one after the other. Read and inspect. Pharaoh responds differently to each one. More importantly, we learn how to respond to God, and how we often respond badly. Moses finally goes from zero to hero.

Prayer focus for this week

Q: The Question — *What is the writer saying?*
A: The Answer — *How Can I apply this to my life?*

Sunday • Exodus 8:16-32

DIGGING DEEPER • Bugs everywhere… biting lice and pesky flies, to be more specific, and not a few. There were swarms of them, and the people didn't have any bug spray, either! By now, even Pharaoh's magicians are saying, This is the finger of God. We know it was miraculous, because the bugs only occurred where the Egyptians lived — not the Israelites. So why doesn't Pharaoh give up? Two reasons: 1) Pharaoh's heart was hardened. 2) God could punish Egypt for enslaving Israel for hundreds of years. Pharaoh partially consented by allowing Moses and Aaron to go a short distance to worship God (vv. 25-32), but not very far. Doing only part of what God wants is like doing none of what He wants. Moses didn't budge.
Half obedience is no obedience. Do you expect God to bless you while you fail to surrender parts of your life? What part should you submit to God?

Monday • Exodus 9:1-12

DIGGING DEEPER • The plagues are getting much more serious. All the livestock (needed for food, milk, transportation, and working animals) are dead – except for those of the Israelites. By now, the land of Egypt is broken. What used to be a beautiful, magnificent land now looks horrible and stinks of death. Then the people get hit with having boils. Interestingly, they take soot (ashes) and throw it into the air. Some think it was from the furnaces which were used for making all the bricks. The very place where Egypt forced slavery upon Israel became the source of Egypt's pain and suffering. My, how things turn around so fast! Don't play games with God like Pharaoh did.
Often the bad things we do come back to haunt us. Is there something you should make right so as not to suffer future consequences?

Tuesday • Exodus 9:13-26

DIGGING DEEPER • Verses 13-16 strike a new attitude on these plagues: This is business! I'm guessing most of us have seen a bad storm before, but nothing compares to this. It destroyed almost all the food that was growing in the fields. Supernatural lightning struck, and then severe hail devastated the land even further. Buildings may have crumbled. The massive statues in Egypt were beaten and damaged from the hail. It was like a circle of judgment around the Israelites, while they remained safe and unaffected. Their trees were green and their plants were still healthy and growing. There was an amazingly obvious difference between Israel and the Egyptians. Another of God's purposes is stated in verse 16. Check it out.
Do people see a difference between you and the unsaved? What are you going to do to help others see that the Lord is important in your life?

Wednesday • Exodus 9:27-35

Q&A

DIGGING DEEPER • Today it almost looked like Pharaoh had a change of heart, but no. It's easy for us to play the same game Pharaoh did. We know the right thing to say when necessary, but we don't do anything about it. We hear a sermon preached, we hear something in youth group, our parents confront us, or our friends catch us in something and then we try to say anything we can to get out of trouble. There's just one thing missing; there's no genuine heart change. Not just a change of words, but a change in the very innermost part of our being. We read something in verse 34 that happens every time we merely give lip service. There's only one way to stop: a genuine heart change.
What sin do you finally need to deal with in your life? Who is the only One who can give you a change of heart? Allow Him to do His work in you.

Thursday • Exodus 10:1-15

Q&A

DIGGING DEEPER • Locusts are like enormous grasshoppers. Now this doesn't sound as bad as the hail, but put an army of a few hundred billion of these things together, and you can actually hear them coming from a long distance! We read that the Egyptians still had some vegetation or plant food left. These little critters ate the last of it. They covered the ground until it was black! Imagine crunching everywhere you walked, and getting these squirmy things stuck in your sandals. Yuck! There were literally hundreds of thousands of people affected by this one man's sin! Pharaoh's officials were begging him to let the people go. Your pride can destroy three things: 1) Others, 2) Your relationships, and 3) You.
Who is close to you that could be negatively affected by your pride? Is there a relationship that you need to mend?

Friday • Exodus 10:16-29

Q&A

DIGGING DEEPER • Solitary confinement in a completely dark place is one of the worst things in prison. Minutes feel like hours. You may have felt alone before, but nothing like this! The Bible says it was darkness you could feel, and it's not like they slept through it. It was like being stuck in the deepest part of the ocean. The amazing thing is that Israel had light where they lived. How do we explain that? If it was that dark, you should be able to see some light from somewhere, but no. This was a supernatural darkness, and it lasted for three days. With this plague, Pharaoh wasn't given any warning as he had been with the others. The Egyptians must have thought it was going to last forever. That's scary!
Are you reaching your friends who are in this kind of spiritual darkness? Whom are you going to seek to reach today?

Saturday • Exodus 11:1-10

Q&A

DIGGING DEEPER • Perhaps you haven't known just how displeased the Lord was with Egypt. It's important to know that the Israelites had been slaves for hundreds of years at this point! They had been oppressed, and who knows how many of them were killed unjustly as slaves? What is more amazing is the change in Moses at this point. Remember how we left him? He was so afraid of Pharaoh that his brother Aaron had to do all the talking. Now Moses has gained some unusual boldness and been filled with a righteous anger over the oppression of his people. God uses him to announce the most severe judgment yet – so severe that it would cause the Egyptians to want to get rid of all the Israelites by setting them free.
Are you changing for God's glory? How can you be bolder for the Lord? Are you passionate for the things of this life, or for God's ways?

qt WEEK 41

Time to leave Egypt! Check out the stuff the Lord does to help Israel remember this time in their lives. This is one of the most amazing places in the Old Testament where Christ is pictured for us. We also start reading this week the most popular, amazing, and true stories in all of history.

Prayer focus for this week

Q: The Question *What is the writer saying?*
A: The Answer *How Can I apply this to my life?*

Sunday • Exodus 12:1-13

DIGGING DEEPER • There are a lot of strange things the Lord asked Israel to do in this passage. Most were to be done quickly, because they were getting ready to leave Egypt in a hurry. This passage is special because it is an awesome picture of Jesus and how he saved us: A lamb was slaughtered – Jesus was called the Lamb of God and was killed. The blood of the lamb showed who belonged to Israel. It's the blood of Jesus that separates us from the world. Israel had to apply the blood to the doorposts in faith, just like we accept Jesus by faith. Israel was set free from Egypt, and we are set free from our sin in Christ. The Jewish Passover literally means the Lord passed over their homes and didn't kill their firstborn. **Have you trusted Christ to save you? If so, take time to thank Him several times today. Pick someone with whom to share Christ this week.**

Monday • Exodus 12:14-24

DIGGING DEEPER • There are a lot of cultural things in these passages. What is yeast, anyway? It is the ingredient in bread that causes it to rise and makes it soft. Most bread you eat today has yeast in it. Yeast isn't bad. God just wanted His people to remember this time when He brought them out of Egypt. The "leaven" was supposed to be removed from every Jewish house. It was a picture of sin – get rid of it! He wanted them to continually remember, whenever they ate that unleavened bread, how He had brought them out of Egypt. It might sound a little weird, but they did it in order to protect the firstborn child in each of their homes, by causing the Lord to pass over their homes.
What do you do to remember how the Lord saved you? Are you willing to obey the Lord and remove the things that are sin (leaven) in your life?

Tuesday • Exodus 12:25-36

DIGGING DEEPER • Most of us have seen the effects of disobedience on people who refuse to follow the Lord. Sometimes we might feel like they deserve it. There should also be a side of us that is saddened to see their sin take them into such a terrible hole without God. It's easy to say, "I would never be that stubborn or fight against God like that." Pharaoh ought to serve as a warning against pride. We need to humble ourselves before God in obedience to Him. Stubborn pride can happen to all of us. That's why we need to do whatever it takes to remember how good the Lord is to save us. Pharaoh's pride had gone so far it brought death to his people. There is always great suffering and loss for those who refuse to listen to God.
What am I being stubborn about with God: a wrong boyfriend or girlfriend, not honoring my parents, not working hard? God opposes the proud.

Wednesday • Exodus 12:37-51

Q&A

DIGGING DEEPER • Some of the Egyptians had intermarried with the Jews. These were called the "mixed multitude." They would eventually create problems, as they were the first to complain about the manna which was given to Israel for daily food (Numbers 11:4). Having a bond or connecting with the unsaved will eventually produce problems. That's why dating the unsaved is not only an unwise move, but one that we have been warned about (2 Cor. 6:14-18). Whenever we think we have a better idea than God's, it's going to spell trouble. Satan sometimes works in subtle ways (like the compromise with the mixed multitude) to keep us from truly following the Lord.
When it comes to dating and other associations, do you feel you have a better idea than God's? Do you need to align yourself with the Word?

Thursday • Exodus 13:1-10

Q&A

DIGGING DEEPER • The Lord wanted Israel to consecrate, or devote, the firstborn of all the animals and people to Him. These were the ones the Lord spared when they were in Egypt. These people and animals were going to be used for His purpose in some way. The festival is the one we read about yesterday, but verse 9 has something specific for all of Israel – and for us – to take to heart. Many Jews placed on their wrists and foreheads little strips of leather with God's Word written on them, but what's more important is the necessity of having God's Word on our lips. The challenge is what's more important to you – your reputation, or having people know that you believe the Bible and are willing to share it?
Do people hear you talk about the Bible? Are you too aggressive with God's Word, or do you share it in love?

Friday • Exodus 13:11-22

DIGGING DEEPER • Ever wonder what God is doing in your life? "Is He really leading me, or am I just on my own down here, trying to figure out what I'm supposed to do?" God was leading Israel very specifically. He kept them away from a country that wanted to do battle with them. Even though God could have strengthened them to win, He was gracious in keeping them away from battle. Verse 21 says God led them by fire at night and a cloud by day. It was very visible, and everybody could see it and have assurance that the Lord was leading them. What about today? Ever wish we had a visible way to see God? We do! His Word! Everything you need for life is right there! The question is...How much do you want it?
It may sound too simple, but how much you want God's leading is directly connected to your time and obedience in His Word! What's your choice?

Saturday • Exodus 14:1-14

DIGGING DEEPER • You are reading about one of the most amazing stories in all of history. It has possibly been retold more than any story ever, and it's all true. This is no movie! Verse 2 says "Turn back." No way did Moses want to go back there. Talk about scary. The Lord's plan for Egypt isn't completed yet. Israel finds itself in a showdown with probably the most formidable army in the world. The amazing person is Moses. He has no trouble speaking now, and his confidence and faith in God are tremendous. Everything around Moses looked bad. The people were ready to give up, the army was awesome, and there was no quick way to escape with two million people. Moses put every ounce of hope in God's "Stand still."
Do you depend on yourself to get out of hard spots? What challenges are you facing about which you need to pray? Do you worry or do you rest?

WEEK 42

Some of the hardest issues for Christians today are answered this week. "I don't see God working." "I wonder if He is really looking out for my good." "I don't see how He is going to work through my difficult situation." This week could settle these questions for you forever! These will be some of your favorite verses.

Prayer focus for this week

Q: The Question — *What is the writer saying?*
A: The Answer — *How Can I apply this to my life?*

Sunday • Exodus 14:15-31

DIGGING DEEPER • God is beginning to perform a new manifestation of His protection for Israel. Real faith always demands that we move forward. We can't just tell God we trust Him; we've really got to hold nothing back in our dependence upon Him. This passage is where the Lord moved between Israel and the Egyptians. He gave immediate protection, and an amazing deliverance. Perhaps it is better described as another marvelous display of God's power and protection. Isn't that how you want to operate for the Lord? Don't you want to see things happen that can only be explained by God's power? If you know Christ, the same power and work is available to you. Is it time to move forward?

What do you need to do to take a step of faith? What challenge do you need to pray about and put into His hands? God's waiting. It's your move.

Monday • Exodus 15:1-13

DIGGING DEEPER • Today is an opportunity to review God's goodness. Just look at the deliverance: Moses being rescued from a basket in the Nile, plagues destroying the land, and culminating with the deliverance at the Red Sea, with all of Israel's enemies destroyed. They now had something worthy to sing about! Lord, I lift Your Name on High is a song we sing, remembering how amazing it is that the Lord saved us. Verses 11-13 are the key for today, and reveal the first part of Israel's song. It's easy to celebrate when things are going well, but do we have this same attitude when things are challenging? These verses are true no matter what we find ourselves facing.
Who or what is sometimes greater to you than the Lord? When was the last time you sang with all your heart to Him, desiring to live what you sang?

Tuesday • Exodus 15:14-27

DIGGING DEEPER • The rest of the song mentions other nations. They have heard how the Lord redeemed Israel out of Egypt. Israel continues to move on. Keep in mind all the amazing miracles they've just seen – even in Egypt. They just marched through the Red Sea and saw the destruction of the Egyptian army. The list goes on. You would think that Israel is now ready to fully trust God. But, after only a few days, when the Lord tests them, we find them grumbling for lack of water. If the Lord could do all He had done, couldn't He take care of water for them? They later found out they were only a short distance from beautiful springs of water. After victory, it's often the little things on which we stumble.
After a victory, be ready to trust the Lord even in the little things. What do you often complain about? Will you pray and leave it in God's hands?

Wednesday • Exodus 16:1-13

Q&A

DIGGING DEEPER • Grumble... Grumble. Complaining is one of those sins with which all of us wrestle. Nothing characterizes Israel at this point in their history more than complaining. "But isn't it OK for them to want food and water?" Of course! The question is whether they are going to trust the Lord for it. The Lord had already proven Himself to them. He could be fully trusted to take care of their needs. He also had a perfect plan of provision for them. The people complained to Moses, but verse 8 shows Whom they were really complaining against. God sees everything we go through, and He wants us to have a joyful life. He wants us to let Him provide exactly what we need, when we need it.
When things become difficult and we complain, we are really complaining at God. What challenge do you need to submit to Him right now?

Thursday • Exodus 16:14-22

Q&A

DIGGING DEEPER • Consider this: Israel failed with the test of water at the end of chapter 15. The Lord provided for them anyway. They failed the test of food yesterday, and the Lord provided for them anyway. The Lord was giving them bread and testing them with it as well. Everyone definitely had enough, but only for that day. They had to wake up the next morning and trust the Lord for it all over again. Many of them didn't, but the Lord provided for them anyway. What about you? It's certainly harder to leave things in the Lord's hands, and trust Him for it, but just as we've been seeing in this whole Book – He always takes care of His people! Even when you don't see how He could work, trust Him – you'll never regret it!
Is there a test the Lord has given you that you recently failed? Look for the tests the Lord gives, and determine to trust Him through it all!

Friday • Exodus 16:23-36

DIGGING DEEPER • What do you believe about God? Do you think He really wants to bless you? The Lord is trying to give Israel a special day during which they don't have to work or gather food, by giving them twice as much food the previous day. He's doing something special for them, above and beyond what they need. Yet many people still won't trust God, even when He's going above and beyond to bless them. The question to answer is this: How did they view God? They didn't see Him as wanting to bless them and provide for their needs. "God isn't good enough to us, we want more." Remember that the Lord will take care of your needs in His time, every time, and even bless you beyond that! Be content with what you have.
Are you willing to trust God for all your needs? Perhaps the Lord is just waiting to give you more, if you'll only trust Him. Why not start today?

Saturday • Exodus 17:1-16

DIGGING DEEPER • The Israelites asked an interesting question in verse seven. Was there anything different between Israel and the other nations? After all God had done for them, the answer was unmistakably, Yes! He was among them. The Lord proves it to them again with this battle they face. In fact, we see how the Lord feels about the Amalekites in verse 14. The Lord already told the Israelites He was going to bring them into their own land – a land that was great for growing crops. It would be the perfect place to raise their families, and He was going to bless them. Ever wonder if the Lord is on your side? As a born-again believer, the answer is an unmistakable, Yes!
Go back and think of all the ways the Lord has blessed you and taken care of you. You can rest in the fact that God is always looking out for you.

qt WEEK 43

This week is amazing. So much of it is about all that God wanted to do for His people. For a while, they were doing great, until…well, you'll see. Bring your imagination this week and picture what it must have been like to be there. This is incredible! What a mighty God we serve! See His goodness this week.

Prayer focus for this week

Q: The Question — *What is the writer saying?*
A: The Answer — *How Can I apply this to my life?*

Sunday • Exodus 19:1-13

DIGGING DEEPER • The Ten Commandments are coming this week, and the Lord is asking the people if they are willing to obey them. If so, the Lord will treasure Israel more than any other nation. Wow! Two things happen today. The Lord shows all the people how special Moses is, and their need to trust his leadership. The second is the revealing of God's holiness. Meeting with God is not like meeting a friend at McDonald's. He is holy and awesome, and has committed Himself to these people. It is a special blessing, and not to be taken lightly. So far, only Moses has spoken with God face to face on the mountain. The Lord wants the people to know who He is. He's holy – awesome – all-powerful – and to be respected.
What is your attitude toward God? Is He just your friend or is He your God? Wouldn't you like to have a relationship with God like Moses had? You can!

Monday • Exodus 19:14-25

DIGGING DEEPER • Make a movie in your mind of what verses 16-20 looked like. It's loud, bright, powerful, overwhelming, frightening, and the very ground you stand on feels like it's going to give way! Moses followed the Lord's instructions about consecrating the people. Imagine after all that work; you finally get to the top of this bellowing mountain, and you're ready to talk to God. The first thing He says is, "Go back down." Spending time with God is serious business. We don't go through the same things Moses did, but our privilege is still just as awesome, as we are able to read His Word and pray to Him… and He hears us! It can change your attitude toward prayer and Bible study if you remember Whom it is you're approaching.
Do you want a mountain-top experience with God? It can happen every time you read His Word! It's not just if you approach Him – it's how.

Tuesday • Exodus 20:1-17

DIGGING DEEPER • Here's a great way to look at the Ten Commandments: Four have to do with our relationship with God, and six have to do with our relationships with others. In order to honor God with our lives, our relationships with Him and others must be correct. You might say, "I've never done these things." Check again. "No other gods before me" means anything you treat as more important than Him. An idol could be sports, friends, or popularity. Do you truly obey and honor your parents? Lying or stretching the truth about things to make yourself look better is sin also. Have you ever wanted something your friends have, or been jealous you don't have an iPod or cell phone? It's always right to examine ourselves before God.
Don't write off something that might be true. Remember, He's a holy, perfect God. He sees right through us. Identify one thing to work on today.

Wednesday • Exodus 24:3-12

DIGGING DEEPER • Whoa! Talk about some weird stuff happening today! Here's the deal with the altars: there were 12 tribes of Israel, and the one leader per tribe gave sacrifices on behalf of his people. Half of the blood was left at the altar; the other half was sprinkled on the people. This represented the tribes' commitment to obey the Ten Commandments. It was the Lord's way of anointing them and helping them to see the seriousness of entering into this relationship of obedience to Him. It's serious decision time, but look at what many of the people were able to do and see afterwards. Verses 9-11 must have been amazing! The Lord is letting more of them get closer to Him. God wants to build a relationship with His people.
When we commit ourselves to Him, He lets us get closer to Him. Are you still at a distance? What area of your life needs to be committed to God?

Thursday • Exodus 24:15-25:9

DIGGING DEEPER • Again, God is taking another step toward His people and trying to get closer to them. Remember, when they left Egypt they plundered the Egyptians. They took literally millions or even billions of dollars in gold and jewelry. These people were loaded! The Lord asked if they would be willing to give a small portion of that to construct a moveable tabernacle for Him to inhabit among them. This same awesome God of power, smoke, lightning, consuming fire, and billowing clouds was willing to come down from the mountain to be with His people. God always wants to come closer to His people. The question is this: What are you willing to do to prove to God that you want to be closer to Him?
What gets in the way of your relationship with God? Would you commit to setting it aside to be closer to Him? He is more satisfying than anything!

Friday • Exodus 25:10-22

DIGGING DEEPER • You'll need to use your imagination as to what this ark looked like. Your pastor might be able to locate a picture of it. It's called the Ark of the Covenant, or Ark of the Testimony. An ark is a container that carries something. Noah's ark carried animals and people. The Ark of the Testimony was a very ornate, gold-covered box measuring 45 inches by 27 inches. It contained the Ten Commandments, engraved on two stone tablets, along with two other items: Aaron's rod that budded, and a pot of manna. The ark was to be carried on the shoulders of men using two long poles placed through rings of gold. The amazing thing is the detailed instructions that the Lord gave for its construction.
These instructions were to be followed carefully, to show respect for God's holiness. What instruction from the Word do you need to heed?

Saturday • Exodus 31:12-32:6

DIGGING DEEPER • The Jews' Sabbath was the last day of the week – our Saturday. We no longer worship on the Sabbath, but rather on the first day of the week, to memorialize Jesus' resurrection. Chapter 32 is almost unimaginable! Things were going so well, and God was blessing the people when they did this. Moses was still on the mountain (a total of forty days) with God during this time. Even Aaron, the one who spoke to Pharaoh along with Moses, went along with these acts. The people were tired of waiting to hear from God. They wanted a god they could see and touch, so they made one of their own… out of gold. It was an idol, something that was forbidden in the very first commandment! How easily we forget.
Do you take matters into your own hands instead of trusting Him? Do you want to know God as He is, or as we think He is? Stay on God's timing.

qt WEEK 44

This week is an incredible look at how God responds to His children. It starts with Israel doing something really stupid and sinful, but it ends with the Lord still wanting to be with them. Let yourself get lost in this last week of Exodus. Don't miss Tuesday. It's the key to understanding how great is our God!

Prayer focus for this week

Q: The Question — *What is the writer saying?*
A: The Answer — *How Can I apply this to my life?*

Sunday • Exodus 32:7-20

DIGGING DEEPER • These people sure have fallen a long way! Why would they do this? One reason is because it was the culture of their day to make false gods and worship them. Today, many Christians follow culture, even to their embarrassment. They follow the present culture in sex, movies, and music that do not honor God, and Internet sites that bring filth into the mind. Then on Sunday they act like everything is okay. Moses threw down the Ten Commandments and broke them, not because he was angry, but because the people had broken their agreement with God! We may not carry little gold statues around with us, but we still carry idols in our hearts. Remember, an idol is anything we treat as more important than God.
How have I broken God's Word lately? Have I asked for forgiveness, and truly desired to change? Take a hard look. What idols are in my life?

Monday • Exodus 33:12-23

DIGGING DEEPER • Wow! This passage is amazing! How would you like a personal invitation to see God? There is no other person in the Bible that was given this kind of invitation. Keep in mind Moses' attitude and actions before God (vv. 13-17). Believe it or not, the Lord has given all Christians this kind of invitation. Maybe we won't see Him like Moses did, but His presence not only goes with us; He lives inside of us! He also reveals Himself to us completely. It happens through His Word. Everything He wants us to know about Him is there. Then why isn't the Christian life as dramatic and exciting for us as it was for Moses? Again, it's his attitude and actions. We are missing the kind of humility and desire that Moses had.
The lack of spending time in His Word reveals a lack of desire and humility. What can you do to change that? Is God your most important passion?

Tuesday • Exodus 34:1-17

DIGGING DEEPER • In today's passage we have a very interesting verbal portrait of God. Sometimes it's hard for us to see Him like this, but it's an accurate description. The Lord was still willing to re-establish His covenant with Israel. Another set of the Ten Commandments was made, and the Lord was willing to be with His people… the very same people who worshipped other gods. But now He gives an even stronger warning regarding idolatry. We are often no different than Israel in how we follow the Lord, but He is faithful and will not forsake us. His blessings on our lives are often directly related to our obedience to Him. Consider this: "I am the only one standing in the way of being closer to God and receiving His blessing."
How can you go deeper in your prayer life and quiet time with Him? What are you doing to make verses 8-9 a part of your life?

Wednesday • Exodus 34:18-35

Q&A

DIGGING DEEPER • The first part of this passage talks about a couple of feasts for the whole nation. The feasts were a time to celebrate and honor God. The people were to remember how He brought them out of bondage in Egypt. Their sacrifices were a means of giving God their best, and trusting that He would bless them even more in the future…and He did. Moses eventually came down the mountain with the second set of the Commandments, but there was something different – Moses' face was glowing! That's wild! Everybody knew that Moses had a special bond with God, and they knew by his countenance that he had just spent quality time with Him. When you have your quiet time, is your countenance changed?
Are you different after you spend time with God? Do people see that you have a special friendship and bond with God? It should be clearly seen!

Thursday • Exodus 40:1-16

Q&A

DIGGING DEEPER • Today we're reading about the tabernacle. It was a moveable place of worship. Remember, Israel is still in the desert, and the whole nation is going from place to place. Each time they move, they are to set up this tabernacle, and then take it down whenever the Lord has them move again. The first place that is described is the Holy of Holies – the innermost part of the tabernacle. It's the place for the gold-laden Ark of the Covenant (Exodus 25:10-22), which holds the Ten Commandments. Verse 16 is the key to this passage. God was going to dwell with His people around the Ark of the Covenant, but in order for them to enjoy God's presence; they had to do things just as the Lord said… that's obedience.
Is there anything in your life in which you are not obeying God? Sin keeps you from getting close to Him. What do you need to do to get closer?

Friday • Exodus 40:17-27

DIGGING DEEPER • There are lots of details explained today, but they are all important. In fact, check out how many times you read, "as the Lord commanded." Verse 21 tells us the Ark of the Covenant had to be shielded. Moses set up another room around the first. The inner room (court), the Holy of Holies, was where God was going to come and live. Going into the Holy of Holies wasn't for everyone – it was only for the high priest, and he had to be purified first. That was the purpose of the outer court. The priest had to be ceremonially cleansed and made pure before entering into God's presence. Verses 22-27 were the things that God used to help the priests become pure. Isn't it amazing that we can come directly to Him?
Prayer is an amazing privilege. Are you taking full advantage of it? Imagine… talking directly with God. What a blessing (Hebrews 4:15-16)!

Saturday • Exodus 40:28-38

DIGGING DEEPER • This is cool! God descended in a cloud of smoke. It was called the Shekinah Glory." Imagine the awesome scene, as an intense funnel of smoke came straight out of the sky and dominated the entire place. God was finally dwelling with His people. We started the Book of Exodus learning how Israel was persecuted in Egypt and cried out to God. Today we see God dwelling with them. Even though Israel was often disobedient, God was on a mission to dwell with them, and He did! That's the Book of Exodus, and possibly also our story. We needed a Savior. God sent us His Son, Jesus. We admitted we were sinners. He saved us, and now He's not just with us – He lives in us. That's awesome!
Whom do you know that needs an Exodus experience with God? Will you be the one to bring him to the Lord? Will you start praying for him now?

qt WEEK 45

Which is easier to read: a letter from someone who is mad at you or a letter from a good friend who wants to give you some practical advice? As Paul writes to his companions in Philippi, you can sense the love between them. This week you will get some very practical advice from our good friend, the Apostle Paul. Read on!

Prayer focus for this week

Q: The Question *What is the writer saying?*
A: The Answer *How Can I apply this to my life?*

Sunday • Philippians 1:1-7

DIGGING DEEPER • "I thought you said you were finished cleaning your room," your mom says as she looks through your bedroom door. "I am finished," you reply. "Finished," she responds, "you call this clean?" Sometimes getting a job done is difficult and we give up halfway through. What if God decided not to finish the work He began in you? What if God decided that He had kept you saved long enough and He was tired of it? It is great to know that that will not happen. The Apostle Paul and Timothy, as they wrote to the Christians at Philippi, reminded them that God was going to finish the work that He began in them (v. 6). They could be confident that God would not give up halfway through. He would finish the job.

How can God's faithfulness encourage you to live a confident Christian life? Having this confidence, how will you be bold for Christ this week?

Monday • Philippians 1:8-14

DIGGING DEEPER • It is scary to think how your life can influence others. Evidently, some of the difficulties that the Apostle Paul had faced were reported to the people of Philippi. Paul reminds them that God can be glorified and others can be impacted through difficulties. Paul says that the difficulties he faced happened so that the Gospel could be shared in many different places (v. 12). In fact, he says that because of his bonds (being in jail), Christ was preached in several places, including the palace. Another result of Paul's difficulties was the influence it had on others. Because Paul was thrown into prison, other Christians were "much more bold to speak the word without fear" because of Paul's influence (v. 14).
How does your life influence others? How can you help others be "more bold" to preach the Gospel?

Tuesday • Philippians 1:15-21

DIGGING DEEPER • What is your passion? Fill in the blank: It doesn't matter what happens, as long as I get to…. what? The Apostle Paul was all about Jesus Christ being lifted up, and about being able to preach the Word of God. He says that different people preach Jesus Christ in different ways. Paul does not worry about the method. He is excited that Jesus Christ is being preached (vv. 15-18). He says that his driving passion ("earnest expectation and my hope") is that Jesus Christ is lifted up, whether Paul lives or dies. To Paul, life is Christ and death is gain (v. 21). Paul's passion was Jesus Christ and Him glorified. Again, what is your passion?
Will you make Jesus Christ your passion? How will you begin to do that today?

Wednesday • Philippians 1:22-30

DIGGING DEEPER • Who is your biggest encourager? Who is the person who helps you become a better person? For the people of Philippi, it must have been the Apostle Paul. Paul had a desire to go to Heaven, but knew that these people needed him to be with them for their morale (vv. 23-24). Paul, however, encouraged them to live a godly life even if he was not around (v. 27). It would have been easy to live godly while the Apostle Paul was present, but Paul wanted their lifestyle to go beyond the have to to the want to. He wanted to be able to hear reports of godly living and unity even if he was not with them. He wanted them to stand on their own two feet spiritually because he knew they would soon face suffering (v. 29).
How do you behave? How can you make your conduct more like that which is appropriate for a Christian?

Thursday • Philippians 2:1-8

DIGGING DEEPER • Have you ever heard the phrase "Like father, like son"? It means that a father and son act alike or think alike because they are related. If you are a Christian, you are now related to Jesus Christ. Your actions should reveal to Whom you are related. Paul says, "Let this mind (attitude) be in you, which was also in Christ Jesus" (v. 5). This entire passage hinges on this verse. If you have the mind of Christ, you will be unified with other believers (v. 2), you will think of others before yourself (vv. 3-4), you will not be puffed up (v. 7), you will be a servant (v. 7), and you will be humble and obedient (v. 8). If you are a Christian, be a Christian (Christ-like). Begin by having the mind of Christ.
How can you have the mind of Christ? What will you do today that will make you think and act more like Christ?

Friday • Philippians 2:9-16

DIGGING DEEPER • What's in a name? Well, "At the name of Jesus every knee should bow…every tongue should confess that Jesus Christ is Lord." The name of Jesus is a precious name. Paul says, "Wherefore," or in other words, "Because it is true that all will bow to the name of Jesus," we should "work out your [our] own salvation with fear and trembling." Work out our salvation? What does that mean? It means since Jesus is Who He is and has saved us from our sin, we should work for Him. We are not working to obtain salvation, but working because we have obtained it. While we are working, we must remember not to complain or murmur (v. 14) so we might shine as lights as we hold forth the word of life (vv. 15-16).
What work (Christian Service) can you do today? How will that work give honor and glory to the name of Jesus Christ?

Saturday • Philippians 2:17-23

DIGGING DEEPER • What kind of reputation do you have with those in your church? In yesterday's passage, we learned that we were to work because we have been saved. Do others know that you work for Jesus Christ? When your name is mentioned at your church, do you have the reputation of one who serves God? Paul decided that Timothy was going to make a trip to visit the people of Philippi. As he discussed the young Timothy in his letter, he drew attention to the reputation that Timothy already had with the church. Paul said, "Ye know the proof of him…he hath served with me in the gospel" (v. 22). The church at Philippi knew that Timothy was a godly man.
What do people think when your name is mentioned? How can you improve your reputation? In what Christian Service will you participate this week?

qt WEEK 46

Paul wrapped up his letter to his friends in Philippi with more practical advice. He wanted this church to live a successful Christian life. To gain wisdom on how to be unselfish, humble, focused, secure, and giving, and to have a godly thought life, read and apply the message of this week's passages.

Prayer focus for this week

Q: The Question — *What is the writer saying?*
A: The Answer — *How Can I apply this to my life?*

Sunday • Philippians 2:24-30

DIGGING DEEPER • Who is the most unselfish person you know? Paul had a good friend and fellow worker named Epaphroditus. Paul said that this guy not only ministered to him in the things that were necessary, but also in the things that Paul wanted (v. 25). Paul reported to the church at Philippi that Epaphroditus had been sick. He was so sick he was about to die. However, God had mercy on him and healed him. Then Paul told the church why Epaphroditus had been sick. He said, "For the work of Christ he was nigh unto death" (v. 30). This guy was so unselfish he almost died ministering to the needs and wants of Paul because the church at Philippi had failed to help Paul (v. 30).

What do you do to help your church grow? How can you use your life to fill the needs or the goals of your church? How can you be more unselfish?

Monday • Philippians 3:1-6

DIGGING DEEPER • Do you know anyone who thinks he is "all that… and more"? Doesn't it make you sick? Paul reminds us that if we ever get to the point where we start bragging about how good we are, we need to think again. Paul had a pretty good religious background (v. 5-6). His background, however, was not what made him a good Christian. Paul says that true Christians "worship God in the spirit…rejoice in Christ Jesus, and have no confidence in the flesh" (v. 3). Our abilities and heritage should not be the center of attention. We must worship the Lord in the spirit, and our rejoicing must be in Jesus Christ, not in our accomplishments.
How will you "worship God in the spirit"? How will you "rejoice in Christ Jesus"? What can you do to decrease so that Christ can increase?

Tuesday • Philippians 3:7-14

DIGGING DEEPER • What goals do you have for your life? What needs to happen in order for you to achieve them? If you are going to achieve any of your goals, you must stay focused on them. In this passage, Paul is the epitome of focus. He considers any accomplishment and every ambition to be worthless compared to knowing Christ (v. 8). He wants to know Christ in His resurrection, in His suffering, and in His death (v. 10). Paul considers himself and his past accomplishments unimportant and stays focused on the prize of the "high calling of God in Christ Jesus" (v. 14).
On what do you focus? Has anything taken your focus off Christ? How will you make Jesus Christ the most important person in your life?

Wednesday • Philippians 3:15-21

Q&A

DIGGING DEEPER • Did you ever play follow the leader when you were younger? The type of leader you had determined what you would do and where you would go. Paul tells the people of Philippi to follow his example. He encourages them to have the same mindset as he had when it came to forgetting the past and pressing on to the future (vv. 15-16). However, Paul does not act like he is the only one doing right. He tells them to "mark" (note) others who live righteously as examples to follow as well. He warns us to stay away from those who walk like the world because our citizenship is not of this world, but of Heaven (vv. 18-20).
Have you been following the example or the advice of ungodly people in any area of your life? If so, will you confess that as sin? How will you follow Christ this week?

Thursday • Philippians 4:1-7

Q&A

DIGGING DEEPER • Do you ever feel insecure? It is an uneasy feeling. Without security and structure anyone would begin to worry. If the world is crashing down, how can anyone not worry? Paul gives some practical advice in the form of a command: "Be careful [anxious] for nothing" (v. 6). In essence Paul says, "Stop worrying about things." Easier said than done, right? Well, Paul knew that, so he gave us a way to stop worrying. Instead of worrying, we should pray, making our requests known to God. The result? We get peace, but not just any peace. We get the peace of God. A peace that Paul says "shall keep (guard) your hearts and minds" (v. 7). The word keep literally means to fortify. Talk about security!
Do you want peace and security in your life? In what situation do you need to stop worrying and begin praying?

Friday • Philippians 4:8-13

Q&A

DIGGING DEEPER • Whatever you do, do not think about a "Big Mac"! "Big Macs" are sold at McDonalds. Do not think about a "Big Mac"! Listen! Stop thinking about a "Big Mac"! What is the easiest way to stop thinking about a "Big Mac"? That's right, think about something else! We should not be thinking about evil things. So Paul gives us eight replacement thoughts (v. 8), reminds the church to follow his example (v. 9), and encourages them to adapt to their circumstances (v. 12). To think only on things that are true, honest, just, pure, lovely, of good report, virtuous, and praiseworthy is a difficult task in today's society. To be content all the time is difficult as well. Paul reminds us that, through Christ, we can do both.
How can you improve your thought life today? In what circumstance do you need to be content? How will you look to Christ today for strength?

Saturday • Philippians 4:14-23

Q&A

DIGGING DEEPER • The Apostle Paul finishes his letter to the church at Philippi with praise. He praises them for how generous they have been in supplying the financial needs that Paul had. When Paul first began doing missionary work, they were the only support he had (v. 15). While he was in Thessalonica, the Philippian believers sent help to him twice (v. 16). Paul made it very clear that he was not interested in getting money but in seeing the Gospel spread around the world. In response to their giving, Paul affirmed the fact that God would in turn supply their need by Jesus (v. 19). Through it all, Paul desired that God would receive all the glory (v. 20).
What sacrifices can you make to help support a missionary? Whom will you support? How much will you give? Will you consider giving not only money but also yourself?

qt WEEK 47

Where or what is the focus of your life? This week the wisest man who ever lived will give you advice. A life that is not centered on God will be purposeless and without meaning. Nothing can satisfy our soul's hunger but God! We challenge you to read through the whole book in one sitting!

Prayer focus for this week

Q: The Question — *What is the writer saying?*
A: The Answer — *How Can I apply this to my life?*

Sunday • Ecclesiastes 1:1-18

DIGGING DEEPER • If you had more power, wealth, knowledge, and wisdom than anyone else, how would you feel? That was Solomon (the author of this book) in his day. Note that with all the wealth and possessions he had, he called it all vanity! The noun vanity does not mean egotistical pride, but futility, meaninglessness, or that which passes without purpose. The main message of this book is that a person who lives life without thinking about God's purpose will end up frustrated and depressed. Generations come and go, but very few people are remembered.

Do you have a purpose in life? God has one for you if you will accept it! Are you frustrated or depressed? Ask God to reveal a job He wants you to do. It may be helping someone else or studying more for your own benefit.

Monday • Ecclesiastes 2:1-11

Q&A

DIGGING DEEPER • What makes you happy? If you could do anything you want without worrying about place, time, or money, what would you do? That's exactly what Solomon got to do. Notice that he sought after and enjoyed entertainment, bodily gratification, accomplishments, and possessions. But look at the result: it wasn't satisfying to him. It created vanity, futility, and was meaningless to him. Why? It had no eternal significance. Nothing passes into eternity except the Word of God and the souls of men. The measure of our eternal perspective is the time and resources we use on the things that will last forever.
Do at least one thing today that will have eternal significance! Look up Psalms 36 and 63 to learn more about our eternal perspective.

Tuesday • Ecclesiastes 2:12-26

Q&A

DIGGING DEEPER • Have you ever thought through something and come to a logical conclusion only to change it later after receiving more information? As Solomon thinks about life he makes some preliminary conclusions. Some of them do not sound quite right until you follow his thought process through to his final conclusions and counsel in chapter 12. If we consider the product of our labor as coming from the hand of God, we can see purpose in our work and enjoy our food and drink. The conclusion Solomon comes to is that the good man receives wisdom, knowledge, and joy while the sinner receives travail, emptiness, and vexation of spirit.
Read through the entire book of Ecclesiastes in one sitting to get the whole picture. Is your view of God the same as is revealed in the Bible?

Wednesday • Ecclesiastes 3:1-14

Q&A

DIGGING DEEPER • Why do you work? Do you want a nice paycheck or more experience? When your work is viewed as part of God's plan, there is purpose and you can enjoy the fruit of your labor. Unless we seek God's wisdom, we cannot know when to do or when not to do many of the things listed in this passage. God has put eternity in our hearts (v. 11), but being human, we can't fully understand it. Therefore, we need to consider our life as a gift from God, rejoice in it, do well, and enjoy the fruit of our labor. Verse 14 tells us that what God does will last forever. Can we add anything to that? Of course not!

Why do you work? When faced with a choice today, ask God for wisdom as to what to do. Think of your salvation with verse 14 in mind!

Thursday • Ecclesiastes 5:1-15

Q&A

DIGGING DEEPER • Did you catch the warnings in this passage? The first one deals with standing in awe of God. It goes back to fearing the Lord and being careful of what we say and where we say it. Have you ever made a vow of dedication or purity to God? A lot of youth groups urge their young people to do this, but sometimes don't give the scriptural warnings against breaking these vows. The other main warning in this passage deals with wealth and possessions. They do not satisfy! They bring about a desire for more possessions until the possessions possess the possessor. They rob the possessor of sleep and peace of mind.

Do you have a true sense of awe in God? Spend time in prayer focusing on exactly Who He is! Do your possessions possess you? Examine Hebrews 13:5, 1 Timothy 6:6-7, and Matthew 6:19-20 to get a godly perspective.

Friday • Ecclesiastes 11:1-10

DIGGING DEEPER • If you could sit and chat with Solomon and ask any question on how to live your life, what would you ask him? The following are examples of wisdom in this chapter. Don't use up all your resources at once; invest some for the future. There are some things that you can't control. Be prepared to take risks. There are many things in life that you'll never be able to fully understand because God's ways are higher than yours. Do a full day's work. Enjoy your youth, but realize that it passes by quickly. However, behave yourself knowing that God will bring every action you do into judgment.
Apply one (or more) of these pieces of wisdom to your life. Think about what you should do differently knowing you will one day face judgment.

Saturday • Ecclesiastes 12:1-14

DIGGING DEEPER • Have you ever thought, "I'll just have fun now while I'm young and serve the Lord later when I'm older"? Many people do, but Solomon warns that the storms of life come too soon. In verses 3-6 he presents an allegory or illustration about what happens to our body as we age. The silver cord may represent vital signs and the golden bowl the head, which houses your brain. The pitcher could be the heart and the wheel, the circulatory system. He closes by pointing out the importance of choosing our words carefully and reminding us that we will face judgment by our Creator for everything we do!
What can you do to serve the Lord today? Do it! Think about what you're going to say or do before you speak or act, knowing every word and action will be judged.

qt WEEK 48

"Excuses, excuses, excuses, that's all I ever hear!" Have you ever heard those words from your mom or dad after they asked you to clean your room, take out the trash, or do your homework . . . and you didn't? This week we'll see why those who reject God's righteousness through Jesus Christ have no excuse.

Prayer focus for this week

Q: The Question — *What is the writer saying?*
A: The Answer — *How Can I apply this to my life?*

Sunday • Romans 1:1-7

DIGGING DEEPER • Paul introduces us to the main character of the entire book of Romans in the first six words of verse 1: it's Jesus Christ. Paul identifies himself as the servant of Jesus Christ, or literally, the slave who chose to be so when he could have gone free. Wow! That's kind of like choosing to stay in high school for a few extra years instead of graduating. It's actually a much greater sacrifice than that. Because of what Christ did for him, Paul wants to serve Him for the rest of his life, for the glory of God. Jesus Christ did the same things for us that He did for Paul. The highlight of what Christ did for us is that He showed us His power by rising from the dead. It's called the Resurrection, proving He is the Son of God. What specific things does Paul tell us that Jesus Christ did for us? What specific things are you doing that show you are His servant?

Monday • Romans 1:8-17

Q&A

DIGGING DEEPER • Did you ever have a friend or family member move away, and you wanted to see them so badly that you prayed and asked God to make it possible for you to go visit them? Paul prayed that God would allow him to visit the Roman believers so that he could support them in their walk with God. He wanted to see them so that together they could be comforted, encouraged, and strengthened by each other's faith. Paul's desire to share the Gospel with those who hadn't yet believed was so strong that he described it as a debt that he owed them. He was committed to preach the Gospel with every ounce of strength he had, because it is God's power for salvation to all who would believe.
Ask God to burden your heart for one Christian friend whom you could encourage, and one unsaved friend with whom you could share the Gospel.

Tuesday • Romans 1:18-32

Q&A

DIGGING DEEPER • Have you ever shared the Gospel with an unbeliever who argued that God couldn't possibly send people to hell if they had never heard the Gospel? Verse 20 makes it very clear that they have no excuse! God's creation speaks loud and clear and tells us that there is a God. If anyone wants to know the Truth, they just have to open their eyes! We're also told that God "gave them up" (vv. 24, 26) and that He "gave them over" (v. 28). That doesn't mean that God gave up on them, but that because they refused to accept God's Truth, He let them go their own way and suffer the consequences. Anyone can know the Truth if they want to.
Do you know someone who is arguing with God? Using this passage, write out your answer to the question "How can God send someone to hell who hasn't heard the Gospel?"

Wednesday • Romans 2:1-16

Q&A

DIGGING DEEPER • Imagine that you are driving your car and every other car on the road is passing you. You decide to go faster, and before you know it, you are being pulled over for speeding. You tell the policeman that everyone else was speeding and, therefore, he shouldn't give you a ticket. Then he tells you, "That's no excuse!" God will judge all men according to His Truth, His standard. He tells those who point their fingers at others who sin, "That's no excuse!" For those who remain "impenitent" (v. 5 – no repentance), they will be judged according to their deeds.

As a believer, how do you know when you are breaking God's law? Have you disobeyed God this week? If so, how can you make it right with Him?

Thursday • Romans 2:17-29

Q&A

DIGGING DEEPER • "Practice what you preach!" Have you ever heard those words before? They are typically used when referring to someone who tells people not to act a certain way, but then acts that way himself. We call that person a hypocrite. Paul was a Jew and he is now talking to the Jews, who were known for their hypocrisy. They argued that they were keeping the Law, when, in fact, they were just going through the motions and actually violating the very law that they taught others. Obedience comes from the heart, not from mere outward conformity.

Write a brief sentence or two that describes your motivation for going to church or having your quiet time. What words would God use to describe your heart? Could anyone legitimately call you a hypocrite? Why?

Friday • Romans 3:1-8

DIGGING DEEPER • Have you ever wondered what it would be like to be the son or daughter of the President? Just think about the places you could go and the things you could do simply because your dad was the President. I don't think you would ever question whether or not your family gave you an advantage over other people. The Jews had that kind of advantage; they were God's chosen people and were given the "oracles" (v. 2), or the very words of God. Yet with all the advantages they had, they still refused to put their faith in Jesus Christ and His promise of salvation. As a result, they will be judged by God for their unbelief.
List the advantages you have as a result of being a child of God. How have you used those advantages to proclaim the Truth of God?

Saturday • Romans 3:9-20

DIGGING DEEPER • Sometimes when unsaved people are presented with the Gospel, and they are told that they are sinners, their response may go something like this: "Sure, I've sinned. Who hasn't? But hey, I'm not that bad. After all, I haven't killed anyone. I do enough good things. It'll come out all right in the end." God's answer is "There is none that seeketh after God . . . there is none that doeth good" (vv. 11-12). In other words, no man will ever seek after God on his own, and no man can ever be good enough to overcome his guilt. Even keeping the Law (commandments) will not justify anyone. The Law is intended to show us how sinful and unrighteous we are, not to make us better.
Put Paul's description of all men into your own words. How does that make you feel? What hope do we have?

qt WEEK 49

Have you ever been so lost that you were overwhelmed by fear and just about to give up hope of ever finding your way, when suddenly someone you knew showed up and rescued you? Last week's study ended with no hope. This week we will learn about God's answer to man's hopelessness!

Prayer focus for this week

Q: The Question — *What is the writer saying?*
A: The Answer — *How Can I apply this to my life?*

Sunday • Romans 3:21-31

DIGGING DEEPER • Debt is a way of life in the United States. If we want something and don't have the money to buy it, we borrow the money and get what we want. Some people have borrowed so much money that they have no hope of ever getting out of debt. Because we are all sinners, we owe God a debt that we can never pay. But God made it possible for our debt to be paid in full by receiving His righteousness through faith in Jesus Christ. It's not about doing the works of the Law, but accepting the blood of Christ as the payment for our sin. This passage contains many theological words directly related to our salvation. Make a list of those words and what they mean. If necessary, use a Bible dictionary to help you with the definitions.

Monday • Romans 4:1-12

DIGGING DEEPER • "I'll believe it when I see it!" That's how we usually respond when something that we believe to be impossible actually happens, but we don't see it. There are some things in life that we just have to accept as true without seeing them, like electricity or gravity. Have you ever seen either one? Of course not, but you believe that they exist, don't you? We can only experience the righteousness of God by believing Him. We can't earn it or get it through Jewish ceremonies like circumcision. Even Old Testament heroes like Abraham and David had to exercise faith and believe in order to receive God's grace and forgiveness. **Is faith really all that is necessary to receive God's righteousness? How do you know? What did you do to be saved? Write out your salvation story and share it with a friend who knows the Lord and with one who doesn't.**

Tuesday • Romans 4:13-25

DIGGING DEEPER • Luke 1:37 tells us, "For with God nothing shall be impossible." That means a man can live for three days in the belly of a great fish (Jonah 1:17), or a baby can be born to a virgin (Luke 1:34-35), or a baby can be born to a one-hundred-year-old man and a ninety-year-old woman (Genesis 17:17). "Nothing" means "nothing"! Abraham didn't "stagger" (v. 20) or doubt God's promise to give him a son, no matter how old he was. As a result, Abraham received God's righteousness. God's righteousness is also available to us because of another seeming impossibility… that Jesus died on the cross and rose from the dead (vv. 24-25). Wow! Because God did the impossible, you and I can believe and be saved! **For what impossible things have you believed God in the past? Make a list of impossible things for which you want to begin to ask God in the future.**

Wednesday • Romans 5:1-11

Q&A

DIGGING DEEPER • The end of any war, whether it was the Revolutionary War, World War I or II, or Desert Storm in Iraq, has always been a cause for celebration because it brought peace and hope to those who were set free from the enemy. For those of us who have been "justified by faith" (v. 1), we now have peace with God. We were once guilty before God and slaves to sin, but are now free and at peace with Him. That peace has also given us access to God anytime we want it. Peace leads to rejoicing and hope, and the pouring out of God's love in our hearts. Talk about a reason for celebration; we've got a whole bunch of reasons to be thankful and give glory to God!
When's the last time you celebrated your peace with God? Write a prayer to God praising Him for setting you free from sin and giving you peace.

Thursday • Romans 5:12-21

Q&A

DIGGING DEEPER • The story of sin entering the human race through Adam and Eve is a familiar one. It might be easy to think that if we could have taken their place in the garden we wouldn't have sinned. The truth of the matter is that we all sinned in Adam, and that means that we would have done the same thing. But just as sin entered the world through one man, so by the obedience of one man, Jesus Christ, all can be made righteous. The sin of one brought death to all and the death of one brought God's grace and forgiveness to all. Sin is powerful and deadly. The gift of salvation is more powerful than sin and brings life.
Think about the sins you've committed in the last week. Write them on a piece of paper, confess them to God (1 John 1:9) and shred them… you have been forgiven!

Friday • Romans 6:1-12

DIGGING DEEPER • Baptism is a picture of our salvation. When we are baptized, we identify with Christ in His death and burial by being put under the water. When we are raised up out of the water, we identify with Him in His resurrection. The picture is that we are buried to sin and raised up to new life in Christ. As believers, we don't have to sin. Talk about hope – this is more than hope; it is freedom from sin; it is victory! Sin can no longer control us because we are alive in Christ.

Have you been baptized? If not, why not? How will you publicly identify yourself with Jesus Christ this week? List one action step you can take to let your friends see the life of Christ in you.

Saturday • Romans 6:13-23

DIGGING DEEPER • What controls you? To what do you give your time each day? Do you play on one of the sports teams in your school or community? Do you play a musical instrument? Do you have a part in the school play? If so, you must commit your time to long hours of practice or rehearsal. You must willingly give yourself to your team and the coach, to your instrument, or to the director of the play. If you want to have victory over sin, you must give your time and effort to doing those things that please God. If you spend your time on things that are not pleasing to God you will become a slave to those things. Remember, "The wages (penalty) of sin is death; but the gift of God is eternal life" (v. 23). Live your life for God!

Is sin controlling you? How? What friends or activities do you need to get rid of? Why? What do you need to do today to give yourself to God?

qt WEEK 50

Do you sometimes struggle with this thing we call the Christian life? Why is it so hard? Why do we do the things that we hate? Why do bad things happen to good people? Why does it seem that at times God is unfair? Why, why, why? You will find some answers this week, but you might also discover some more questions!

Prayer focus for this week

Q: The Question — *What is the writer saying?*
A: The Answer — *How Can I apply this to my life?*

Sunday • Romans 7:1-13

DIGGING DEEPER • Have you ever been to a wedding? Did you actually listen to what the pastor said when he asked the bride and groom to repeat their vows? Do you remember the part about "for as long as you both shall live" and "until death do us part"? That means that the only thing that should end a marriage is death. And just as death is the only thing that ends a marriage, so our relationship with Christ is the only thing that can make us dead to the law. Once we are dead to the law, we are no longer bound to or controlled by the law, but are set free to live and serve in the Spirit.

Marriage changes your life. How has your salvation, your marriage to Christ, changed your life? Share three specific examples.

Monday • Romans 7:14-25

DIGGING DEEPER • Count how many times the word I is used in these verses. That's right, a lot. "For the good that I would I do not: but the evil which I would not, that I do" (v. 19). What in the world is Paul trying to tell us?… I, I, I… me, me, me. Even as a believer, Paul identifies himself as "carnal" (v. 14). Carnal means subject to the weaknesses of the human flesh. Even though we are saved and don't have to sin, the struggle against sin still exists. It sounds like Paul is almost ready to give up and give in to sin when he exclaims, "O wretched (miserable) man that I am! Who shall deliver me" (v. 24)? Is there any hope? Yes, it is through Jesus Christ our Lord!

When do you struggle most to overcome sin? What sin do you struggle with the most? Are you focused on "I" or on Jesus Christ, our Lord?

Tuesday • Romans 8:1-11

DIGGING DEEPER • I'm sure you've seen the TV shows that take place in the courtroom. The evidence is presented and the jury decides the guilt or innocence of the defendant. If the words "not guilty" are heard, everyone shouts for joy and celebrates because there is "no condemnation" for the defendant. The words "no condemnation" are also true for everyone who is in Christ Jesus. We have been set free from sin and death because God's own Son became our sin offering. We can now live in the power of the Spirit of God because we have been forgiven and made alive!

How do you celebrate the fact that we cannot be condemned? What part does the Spirit play in our salvation and spiritual growth?

Wednesday • Romans 8:12-25

Q&A

DIGGING DEEPER • "Hi, Mom" are the famous words we often hear when someone gets in front of a TV camera. Why "Mom," and not "Dad"? Maybe it's because Mom gave birth, and not Dad. For those of us who have been made alive by Christ Jesus and led by the Spirit, we are now "sons of God" (vv. 14-15). We have entered into a new relationship because we have been adopted into the family of God and now cry out "Abba, Father" (v. 15), or in today's language, "Daddy!" As God's children, we have been given an inheritance and a hope for the present and the future. One day God's glory will be revealed in us as we stand in His presence for all eternity.

How would you rate your relationship with your heavenly Father? Do you know Him well enough to call Him "Daddy" when you pray? Why?

Thursday • Romans 8:26-39

Q&A

DIGGING DEEPER • What do you say to someone who has just experienced the death of a friend or family member? In our desire to help, we may say something insensitive or ignorant. Sometimes, the grief is so deep that we don't know what to say. We may not even know how to pray for hurting people. That's when the Holy Spirit "intercedes" for us by taking our groanings and unspoken words to our Father on our behalf. It's during those times that we usually ask "Why did this happen?" The answer is that God works "all things" together to accomplish His will and purpose in our lives. We may not understand what that purpose is, but we can be confident that God will use it for our good and to bring glory to Himself.

Is there hurt in your life today? Are you facing difficult circumstances and wondering what to do? Go to God now and cry out to Him for wisdom.

Friday • Romans 9:1-16

DIGGING DEEPER • How much do you know about Israel? What about Palestine? What is all the fighting about in the Middle East? The Jews are still God's chosen people even though God has turned His attention to the church during this present age. Paul's heart is broken for his fellow countrymen, the Jews. They have rejected Christ as the Messiah and Paul wishes that he could be "accursed" (v. 3) for them. In other words, he is willing to take their eternal punishment in hell if it would mean that they would be saved. Jacob and Esau are mentioned to illustrate God's truth about election. God loved (chose) Jacob and hated (rejected) Esau. Though it's difficult to understand, don't be afraid to study election. It is in the Bible.
How burdened is your heart for your unsaved friends? How much would you do to reach them for Christ? When will you do it?

Saturday • Romans 9:17-33

DIGGING DEEPER • "That's not fair!" is a phrase that comes out of our mouths when someone gets something that we don't get, and we view it as preferential treatment. It might be a complaint verbalized by teens to parents, by students to teachers, or by believers to God. God shows mercy to whomever He wants to show mercy, and He hardens whomever He wants to harden. When we see God's mercy shown to one and not another, we may think that's unfair. But Paul asks, "Who do we think we are" (v. 20)? God is the potter and we are the clay, and the clay can never question the potter's right to do what he wants with the clay! Ultimately, God does what He does to bring glory to Himself, and fairness is never the issue.
Have you been angry at God for treating you or someone else unfairly? Why? What do you need to change about how you think about God?

qt WEEK 51

We begin this week with two of the most used salvation verses in the entire Bible: Romans 10:9-10. God's righteousness for all men, Jew or Gentile, comes only by believing and confessing. Once we're saved, the reasonable outcome is to present our bodies as a sacrifice to God and to serve Him and one another.

Prayer focus for this week

Q: The Question — *What is the writer saying?*
A: The Answer — *How can I apply this to my life?*

Sunday • Romans 10:1-13

DIGGING DEEPER • Numbers 25 tells the story of God's judgment on Israel's sexual immorality. Right in the middle of God's judgment and in front of the entire nation, an Israelite man brought a Midianite woman into his tent to have sexual relations with her. Phinehas was so angered by their sin that he followed them into the tent and thrust a javelin through both of them. God called Phinehas zealous for his God. His zeal was based on knowledge. Romans 10:2 tells us that Israel has zeal for God "but not according to knowledge." Being ignorant of God's righteousness, they zealously tried to earn their own. But God's righteousness comes only by believing in our heart and confessing with our mouth the Lord Jesus as Savior.
Whom do you know who is zealous (excited) about his religion, but wrong? What knowledge can you give them that will lead them to righteousness?

Monday • Romans 10:14-21

Q
A

DIGGING DEEPER • Jesus tells us in Matthew 9:37-38 that the "harvest truly is plenteous (great), but the labourers are few." There is a huge need for people to give themselves to lifetime ministry and take the Gospel into the worldwide harvest. Paul tells us that those in need of the Gospel can't believe if they never hear, and they can never hear if someone doesn't preach to them. It's real simple; faith (the ability to believe) can only come as the lost (the great harvest field of people who don't know the Lord Jesus) hear the Word of God. And they can only hear it if we are willing to take it to them.
What are you doing to reach the world for Christ? Maybe you should Go! Will you seriously consider and pray about a career in missions?

Tuesday • Romans 11:1-12

Q
A

DIGGING DEEPER • Did you see the headline in the leading newspaper? It read, "God Rejects the Nation of Israel!". . . No, not really, but today's text begins with a question that could easily be turned into a major news story, if it were true. However, God has not rejected His people, the Jews. Unfortunately, it is true that Israel rejected Jesus as the Messiah and continued to try to gain their own righteousness by the works of the Law. As a result God put them aside for a time to work with the Gentiles, now known as the church or the bride of Christ. He will turn to them again during the Tribulation period and give them another opportunity to respond favorably to Him by placing their faith and trust in Him.
What can people see in your life that indicates you have not rejected Jesus Christ as the Messiah?

Wednesday • Romans 11:13-24

DIGGING DEEPER • Have you ever read a passage of Scripture like today's passage, struggled to understand it, read it a second time, and then wondered what it really meant? Today's text requires some thought, prayer, and study. The Gentiles (v. 13) are the church and Paul's "flesh" (v. 14) is the Jews. The "firstfruit" and "root" (v. 16) refer to the start of Israel through Abraham, Isaac, and Jacob. The branches that are "broken off" (v. 17) are the Jews who rejected Jesus as Messiah, and "the wild olive tree" (v. 17) is the church. God treated the Jews with "severity or sternness" because of their unbelief, and us with "goodness" because of our faith (vv. 20, 22). Our response ought to be one of fear, humility, and ultimately thanksgiving for our salvation!
When you think of what God has done for you, how do you respond?

Thursday • Romans 11:25-36

DIGGING DEEPER • Most everyone likes a good mystery. Whether it's a book, a TV show, or video, it's always a challenge to work through the plot and try to figure out "whodunit." In 11:25, the "mystery" (something not revealed in the Old Testament) is that God would set aside Israel for a time to work with the Gentiles (the church) until the "fullness of the Gentiles" is complete. This is a reference to the entire number of Gentiles that God intends to save as part of the church. When the last Gentile is saved, Jesus Christ will return for His church at the Rapture and the seven years of Tribulation will begin.
How do you know that you are ready for the Rapture? Knowing that the Rapture can happen at any moment, how does that influence the way you are living right now?

Friday • Romans 12:1-8

DIGGING DEEPER • Can you remember a time when you wanted to get even with someone because of what he did to you? Have you ever thought about getting even with God, because of what He did for you? Now, we can never really get even with Him or pay Him back because of all that He has done for us. But we can "present (or offer) our bodies a living sacrifice" (v. 1) to God, because of His mercies, so that He can accomplish His will in our lives. When we take that "reasonable" (v. 1) or spiritual step, we are then ready to use the "gifts" (special God-given abilities for service - v. 6) to minister to other members of the body of Christ.
What are you doing now because of the "mercies of God" in your life? What "gifts" has God given you for serving Him? How are you developing and using those gifts?

Saturday • Romans 12:9-21

DIGGING DEEPER • "They're all a bunch of hypocrites!" That's a phrase that is sometimes used by people in reference to the church, in an attempt to cover up their own bad behavior. However, we as believers do sometimes act like hypocrites. Paul gives us a list of practical tips for daily living that will reflect the righteousness of God in our lives. The list begins with love. Love is not hypocritical. "Dissimulation" (v. 9) is the word for hypocrisy. It comes from the ancient Greek theatrical practice of having actors wear masks for different parts in the play and, as a result, hiding their true identity. It means, not speaking from under a mask in order to deceive. If we learn to "love one another" first, the rest of the list will be easy.
Are you a hypocrite? Why? What do you need to change? Which three items in this list do you struggle with the most? How will you improve?

qt WEEK 52

Life is all about relationships! In fact, after telling us to love the Lord with all our heart, Jesus tells us to "love thy neighbour as thyself" (Matthew 22:39). This week we will learn about the value of people and how to live at peace with all men whether saved or unsaved, weak or strong, Jew or Gentile.

Prayer focus for this week

Q: The Question — *What is the writer saying?*
A: The Answer — *How Can I apply this to my life?*

Sunday • Romans 13:1-14

DIGGING DEEPER • Periodically, a country elects a new political leader, and whether or not we agree with the outcome of the election, we are to submit to the government that God has established. The key is to remember that God is sovereign and the ultimate authority in our country. We are to obey our earthly rulers, not only because of the fear of punishment, but also because of our conscience before God. We keep the law by obeying the speed limit, not shoplifting, and telling the truth. But we also keep the law by loving our neighbor like we love ourselves. When we love our neighbor that way, the rest of the commandments will take care of themselves.

How often do you pray for our elected officials? Why do you obey the law? Who are your neighbors? What are you doing to love them?

Monday • Romans 14:1-12

Q
A

DIGGING DEEPER • The lyrics to the popular worship song Jesus, Lover of My Soul (It's All About You), could be the theme song for today's passage. The song begins with, "It's all about You, Jesus" and continues, "It's not about me. . ." If we could learn to put those words into action on a daily basis, we would never think of "despising" or judging one another (vv. 3-4, 10). These verses deal with the gray areas of life. The specific issue at hand is whether or not a Christian should eat meat offered to idols. One believer eats and one (weak brother - new or immature believer) doesn't. Neither is wrong nor is either to judge the other. Both are to live for the Lord, because God is the judge and will hold each one accountable.
What gray areas do you argue about with other Christians? Are you critical of them? What Biblical basis do you have for the things that you believe?

Tuesday • Romans 14:13-23

Q
A

DIGGING DEEPER • If your mom made dinner tonight with meat that had been offered to idols, would you eat it? Now, that's probably not a realistic possibility. But what if viewing a decent video in front of one of your friends would cause him to stumble (vv.13, 21) or more literally, to sin; would you view it anyway? Now you might think, "That's ridiculous. What's wrong with viewing a video? Viewing isn't a sin!" No it's not, unless the weaker believer considers it questionable and that causes him to sin. A bit extreme? Maybe, but it's exactly the kind of thing that Paul is talking about. Whatever the issue, let's not "destroy" (v. 15) our brother by doing what we think is okay. We need to pursue things that lead to spiritual growth.
What are you doing that leads to the spiritual growth of other believers? What activity would you give up for the sake of a weaker brother?

Wednesday • Romans 15:1-16

Q&A

DIGGING DEEPER • Would you consider yourself to be a weak or a strong believer? Most of us would like to think that we are strong, but how do we know for sure? Paul gives us a foolproof test. Those who are strong "ought to" or actually are duty-bound to "bear the infirmities (weaknesses) of the weak" (v. 1) and to "please his neighbour for his good" (v. 2). It couldn't be clearer. Mature believers are to live for the glory of God and the good of others, for even Christ chose not to please Himself. We are to accept one another just as Christ accepted us, and be likeminded (v. 5) toward each other.
Does God consider you to be a strong believer? What are you doing to please your neighbor in school, at work, in your youth group? How have you specifically chosen not to please yourself for the good of a brother?

Thursday • Romans 15:17-33

Q&A

DIGGING DEEPER • Ben Franklin said, "It's amazing what can be accomplished when no one cares who gets the credit." We live in a society that makes a big deal about who gets the credit. Paul was greatly used of God to take the Gospel to the Gentiles, from Jerusalem to central Europe, and all the way to Spain. He was an amazing servant of God. He cared that people heard the Gospel and that God got the credit and the glory for all that he was able to accomplish. Paul's request for the prayers of the Roman church for his ministry in Jerusalem and Judea, including his trip to Rome, indicates his dependence on God. When we learn to depend on God, we also learn that He deserves the credit for all that takes place.
What is God doing in your life for which you are taking the credit? What more could you do if you cared only that God got the credit?

Friday • Romans 16:1-16

DIGGING DEEPER • Do you remember this week's overview? Relationships have been at the heart of everything that Paul has said in the last four chapters of his letter to the church at Rome. Are you a friendly person? Paul was. As a result, he had a lot of friends. He greets twenty-eight people by name in chapter 16. He didn't just know their names, but in many cases, he knew very specific details about them. This only comes through spending time with them. It would also seem to indicate that he didn't seek to please himself, but had actually built some lasting relationships with them and sought to encourage his brothers and sisters in Christ everywhere he went.
How well do you know the people in your church? What are you doing to get to know them so that you can pray for them specifically and by name?

Saturday • Romans 16:17-27

DIGGING DEEPER • Paul closes the last section of his letter with a warning to mark, or watch out (v. 17), or keep an eye on those who cause divisions within the church that are contrary to the doctrines they have been taught, and to stay away from them. Relationships with disobedient people can be devastating to the church and the testimony of Jesus Christ. Paul ends his letter the way he began it - with an emphasis on the grace of God and the person of the Lord Jesus Christ. We would do well to make sure that there is always a constant emphasis on the grace of God and the Lord Jesus Christ in our lives!
Are you spending time with those who are living contrary to the Truth of the Word of God? Why? What does the grace of God mean to you? How does your life reflect the presence of the Lord Jesus Christ?

The following chart is provided to enable everyone using Word of Life Quiet Times to stay on the same passages. This list also aligns with the daily radio broadcasts.

week 1	Aug 26 – Sep 1	Psalms 26:1-31:24
week 2	Sep 2 – Sep 8	Psalms 32:1-35:28
week 3	Sep 9 – Sep 15	Psalms 36:1-39:13
week 4	Sep 16 – Sep 22	Psalms 40:1-45:17
week 5	Sep 23 – Sep 29	Psalms 46:1-50:23
week 6	Sep 30 – Oct 6	2 Corinthians 1:1-4:18
week 7	Oct 7 – Oct 13	2 Corinthians 5:1-8:24
week 8	Oct 14 – Oct 20	2 Corinthians 9:1-13:14
week 9	Oct 21 – Oct 27	Genesis 1:1-5:32
week 10	Oct 28 – Nov 3	Genesis 6:1-11:9
week 11	Nov 4 – Nov 10	Genesis 12:1-22:18
week 12	Nov 11 – Nov 17	Genesis 24:1-27:33
week 13	Nov 18 – Nov 24	Genesis 27;34-35:15
week 14	Nov 25 – Dec 1	Genesis 37:1-41:36
week 15	Dec 2 – Dec 8	Genesis 41:37-44:34
week 16	Dec 9 – Dec 15	Genesis 45:1-50:26
week 17	Dec 16 – Dec 22	Matthew 1:1-4:25
week 18	Dec 23 – Dec 29	Matthew 5:1-7:29
week 19	Dec 30 – Jan 5	Matthew 8:1-10:31
week 20	Jan 6 – Jan 12	Matthew 10:32-12:50
week 21	Jan 13 – Jan 19	Matthew 13:1-15:39
week 22	Jan 20 – Jan 26	Matthew 16:1-19:15
week 23	Jan 27 – Feb 2	Matthew 19:16-22:33
week 24	Feb 3 – Feb 9	Matthew 22:34-24:51
week 25	Feb 10 – Feb 16	Matthew 25:1-26:56
week 26	Feb 17 – Feb 23	Matthew 26:57-28:20

week 27	Feb 24 – Mar 1	James 1:1-3:10
week 28	Mar 2 – Mar 8	James 3:11-5:20
week 29	Mar 9 – Mar 15	Proverbs 6:1-8:11
week 30	Mar 16 – Mar 22	Proverbs 8:12-10:32
week 31	Mar 23 – Mar 29	1 Chronicles 10:13-17:27
week 32	Mar 30 – Apr 5	1 Chronicles 21:18-29:30
week 33	Apr 6 – Apr 12	2 Chronicles 1:1-7:11
week 34	Apr 13 – Apr 19	2 Chronicles 7:12-20:30
week 35	Apr 20 – Apr 26	2 Chronicles 29:1-36:21
week 36	Apr 27 – May 3	1 Peter 1:1-3:7
week 37	May 4 – May 10	1 Peter 3:8-5:14
week 38	May 11 – May 17	Exodus 1:1-4:17
week 39	May 18 – May 24	Exodus 4:18-8:15
week 40	May 25 – May 31	Exodus 8:16-11:10
week 41	Jun 1 – Jun 7	Exodus 12:1-14:14
week 42	Jun 8 – Jun 14	Exodus 14:15-17:16
week 43	Jun 15 – Jun 21	Exodus 19:1-32:6
week 44	Jun 22 – Jun 28	Exodus 32:7-40:38
week 45	Jun 29 – Jul 5	Philippians 1:1-2:23
week 46	Jul 6 – Jul 12	Philippians 2:24-4:23
week 47	Jul 13 – Jul 19	Ecclesiastes 1:1-12:14
week 48	Jul 20 – Jul 26	Romans 1:1-3:20
week 49	Jul 27 – Aug 2	Romans 3:21-6:23
week 50	Aug 3 – Aug 9	Romans 7:1-9:33
week 51	Aug 10 – Aug 16	Romans 10:1-12:21
week 52	Aug 17 – Aug 23	Romans 13:1-16:27